OUR FOUNDERS' WISDOM

DAVID P. MCINTYRE

B **BENNETT**
MEDIA & MARKETING

All Biblical references are from the New King James Bible (NKJB)

Our Founders' Wisdom

Copyright © 2024 by David P. McIntyre

Bennett books may be ordered through booksellers or by contacting:

Bennett Media and Marketing
1603 Capitol Ave., Suite 310 A233
Cheyenne, WY 82001
www.thebennettmediaandmarketing.com
Phone: 1-307-202-9292

ISBN: 978-1-957114-99-6 (softcover)
ISBN: 978-1-964296-00-5 (eBook)

Printed in the United States of America

Signers of the Declaration of Independence[1]	Nelson Jr., Thomas	Read, George
	Paca, William	Bassett, Richard
Adams, John	Paine, Robert Treat	Spaight, Richard Dobbs
Adams, Samuel	Penn, John	Blount, William
Bartlett, Josiah	Read, George	Williamson, Hugh
Braxton, Carter	Rodney, Caesar	Jenifer, Daniel
Carroll, Charles of Carrollton	Ross, George	King, Rufus
Chase, Samuel	Rush, Benjamin Dr.	Gorham, Nathaniel
Clark, Abraham	Rutledge, Edward	Dayton, Jonathan
Clymer, George	Sherman, Roger	Carroll, Daniel
Ellery, William	Smith, James	Few, William
Floyd, William	Stockton, Richard	Baldwin, Abraham
Franklyn, Benjamin	Stone, Thomas	Langdon, John
Gerry, Elbridge	Taylor, George	Gilman, Nicholas
Gwinnett, Button	Thornton, Matthew	Livingston, William
Hall, Lyman	Walton, George	Paterson, William
Hancock, John	Whipple, William	Mifflin, Thomas
Harrison, Benjamin	Williams, William	Clymer, George
Hart, John	Wilson, James	FitzSimons, Thomas
Hewes, Joseph	Witherspoon, John	Ingersoll, Jared
Heyward Jr., Thomas	Wolcott, Oliver	Bedford, Gunning, Jr.
Hooper, William	Wythe, George	Brearley, David
Hopkins, Stephen		Dickinson, John
Hopkinson, Francis	**Signers of the US Constitution[2]**	Blair, John
Huntington, Samuel		Broom, Jacob
Jefferson, Thomas	Washington, George	
Lee, Francis Lightfoot	Franklin, Benjamin	**First Supreme Court Justices[3]**
Lee, Richard Henry	Madison, James	
Lewis, Francis	Hamilton, Alexander	John Jay
Livingston, Philip	Morris, Gouverneur	James Wilson
Lynch Jr.,Thomas	Morris, Robert	John Rutledge
McKean, Thomas	Wilson, James	William Cushing
Middleton, Arthur	Pinckney, Chas. Cotesworth	John Blair Jr.
Morris, Lewis	Pinckney, Chas	Robert Hanson Harrison
Morris, Robert	Rutledge, John	
Morton, John	Butler, Pierce	
	Sherman, Roger	
	Johnson, William Samuel	
	McHenry, James	

---

[1] Signers of the Declaration of Independence | National Archives

[2] Signers of the US Constitution – System (uslegal.com)

[3] Who were the first six Supreme Court justices? | Constitution Center

TABLE OF CONTENTS

I would like to thank my family and friends that helped me in writing this book. They provided valuable insights and gave advice on better ways to say things. I especially want to thank my precious wife who put up with a lot of reading and rereading, a task that she does not particularly enjoy. I would like to thank Amy, our daughter, for some good insights on how to improve the book. A special thank you to Drew and Jill Jones who were willing to tell me straight out the things they did not like including the original title. A special thanks to John Beeler who made suggestions that added some historical garnish to the manuscript. Those things were changed, and the book is better for it. I would like to thank Don King, Rick Weber, my brother Dennis McIntyre, Harvey Johnson, Kris, and Ginny Karelius for their encouragement and pointing out some grammatical errors. Thank you all.

David P. McIntyre

CHAPTER 1
EXPERTS

Becoming One

What does talk about experts have to do with the Wisdom of our Founding Fathers? Everything, because we get our information from others. We trust that the information they give us is correct. We tend to believe what our close friends and those who we respect tell us. If the news reports a story, we tend to accept what is said as fact. If someone tells us a story about another person, we often believe it is true unless we know that it is not true. If we do not know about something, we tend to believe others who appear to speak confidently about a subject. We grant them "expert" status whether they deserve it or not.

What makes an expert? Is it because they have an opinion about something? Is it because they feel strongly about a subject? Is it because they seem to talk better, more fluently, with bigger, better vocabulary? Is it because they have a charismatic personality and are really good looking as well? The answer is NO. An expert is someone who has studied a subject over a long period of time. That does not mean just watching or listening; it means observing, testing, being very involved with the subject in a personal way. There was a TV ad once illustrating a person with a medical problem lying on the floor. A second person steps up, tells everyone else to step back, and that they will take care of the problem. The second person claims they know what to do because "They have watched a lot of medical dramas on TV". Would the person requiring assistance feel very confident that the person trying to help was an expert because they had watched medical dramas?

Would you feel safe flying with someone who has read books about flying but has never flown? Would it inspire confidence in you, if surgery was about to be performed on you by someone who has never picked up a scalpel? To gain expertise, you have to study and be intimately involved with the subject. In many cases, that means hands on. A surgeon learns surgery by performing surgery under careful guidance by those who are much more knowledgeable. A pilot learns to fly by flying. A mechanic learns to fix engines by studying and fixing engines. Expertise comes through study, observation, hands on approach, training, and guidance which leads to knowledge. It also usually involves some credentials that support the claim to be an expert. It may be a degree in the subject, a certification, or a license to demonstrate to others that they have the knowledge and expertise required for their field. It never is just a claim.

A person who is an expert in something, does not mean that they are experts in everything. Years ago, I had a mild heart attack and sought the advice of a cardiologist. He had the degrees and my wife, who is a nurse, recommended him. He was an expert in caring for the heart. If he spent time advising me about my heart, I listened. If he wanted tests done, I did them. If he prescribed medication, I took them. On the other hand, if I had a problem with my car, I would not go to my cardiologist to seek advice on fixing it. That is not his expertise. As part of my job, I have taught many doctors and PhDs. When they spoke from their expertise, I listened. On other subjects, however, I found they had no more knowledge than the average person on the street. Can we assume that because someone has knowledge in one area that they are also knowledgeable in another?

Our son is a mechanic and has some certifications. He took an engine out of a 1997 Ford Explorer. He tore that engine apart so that every single part of that engine was laid out on my garage floor. He then systematically and carefully replaced every damaged part. He put in new rings, bearings, pistons, and other parts to completely rebuild that engine. He never wrote anything down as he took it all apart, but he remembered where every single nut, bolt, wire, and part went. He and his son put it all back together and dropped the engine back into the SUV. He put the key in the ignition and the engine started almost immediately. It sounded a bit rough at first but once the oil completely circulated throughout the engine, it sounded much better. When he revved it up, it sounded like a powerful racing engine ready to eat up the nearest racetrack. He clearly demonstrated that he was an expert in certain engines. Now when we have a problem with our cars, we ask his advice. I do not ask his advice about my heart. That is not his expertise. Later on, he decided to rebuild the transmission in that Explorer. He was smart enough to realize that while he could rebuild the engine, he did not know enough to rebuild the transmission. He opted to take it to a transmission place that did have the expertise. Our grandson has now driven that SUV for over three years.

Facts Not Emotion

Should we grant expert status to others based on emotion? If we are angry with someone, for example, we will often listen to someone who will fuel that anger. How many times has our dislike for someone made us more susceptible to believing stories against that person? Riots, destruction, vigilante mentality are all fueled by emotion.

Does emotion clarify or distort the facts? Does an angry person want the facts or their pound of flesh, revenge, or someone to blame? The charismatic leader who stirs up the crowd is given expert status. Is that right? History is full of examples of such people and the world has suffered for it. Consider Hitler who stirred up crowds to the point that countries were invaded, people's rights were taken away, and many were simply killed because Hitler said they should be. Recently the news reported a story about group blaming the Jews for the Covid pandemic. Does that really make sense? Many of the Jews, like everyone else, have succumbed to that same pandemic. People just want someone to blame. Are we blaming too much rather than accepting facts or responsibility?

Some Things Have No Experts

If certain subjects cannot be studied, can there be any experts on those subjects? That might be considered a radical thought because we would like to think that we can conquer anything and master everything. Experience has shown there are definite limits to what can be known.

Can we determine, for example, if there is life on another planet outside our solar system? The nearest star to us is Alpha Centauri located approximately four-and-one-half light years away from us. That means that a beam of light starting from Earth would take four and a half years to travel to that star. No one has ever been there. It is too far away. The maximum speed reached by spacecraft is about 200,000 miles per hour or about 60 miles per second in round figures. The speed of light is about 186,000 miles per second. If human beings were to travel at the maximum speed man has achieved, it would take about 13,950 years to reach Alpha Centauri! Other stars and whole galaxies may be thousands, millions, or even further light years from us than Alpha Centauri. How can anyone study in detail a distant star? We learn some things, but not to the detail that my cardiologist can study the heart and circulatory system, or our son can know a car engine. There are stories about wormholes to distant stars but keep in mind they are just that, stories. No one has ever traveled through a wormhole. Are they even possible?

Planets are considerably smaller than the star it encircles. The planets do not radiate light of their own like the star. They only reflect light from the star. The star itself is just a point of light in the sky. Distant stars can only be seen with the aid of very powerful telescopes. How then can we really study a planet in detail revolving around the star? What observers can do is watch the movement of the star. If there is an apparent wobble, scientists might conclude that there is source of gravitational pull close to the star. With a little math, they might further deduce the approximate strength of the gravitational pull. They cannot tell, however, the source of the gravitational pull or how close the object is to the star. They can only say there appears to be something there. The rest is storytelling.

They cannot say an earthlike planet exists, at the right distance from the star, and life exists on that planet.

Experts or Storytellers

Movies today would have us believe that travel to distant parts of the universe will be possible. Star Trek and Star Wars movies tell us of weird alien beings in distant galaxies with unusual abilities and powers. They tell us of galaxy class ships able to transcend the speed of light to reach and explore them with powerful defense weapons. The movies are fun and enjoyable. There is adventure, edge of your seat action, good versus evil, and usually, after difficult circumstances, the good guys win in the end. They are immensely creative. We must remember, though, they are stories. The books on which they are all based would be found in the libraries under the category "Fiction". They are not established facts. Some of the things portrayed in them certainly might eventually become reality. In early versions of space stories, for example, they envisioned computers that would respond to voice commands. Now it is a reality as computers have evolved. Not all portrayals are guaranteed to become fact. Many are just fanciful creations of a creative mind and may even violate the science we do know.

Does everything portrayed in the movies always reflect what is possible? Captain Picard in Star Trek is often seen giving the order to move the ship forward with the command "Engage". Almost instantly the ship then travels at some speed. A relatively slow speed would be ¼ impulse power. That speed according to Wikipedia, translates into about ¼ the speed of light. Light travels at 186,000 miles per second so ¼ light speed is 46,500 miles per second. Anyone who has ever driven a car knows that when you press hard on the accelerator, you are pushed back in your seat. The greater the acceleration, the harder the push back, also known as g-force. Videos have been made of astronauts showing their faces contorted as they experience the g-forces associated with the rocket acceleration into space. Accelerating from 0 to 46,500 miles per second would produce horrendous g-forces. A proper portrayal of that acceleration would have everyone on the ship squished against the rear bulkhead of the ship a split second after Picard says "Engage". When the ship is brought to a sudden stop, everyone should now be squished against the forward bulkhead. Of course, there is also the problem that the ship could not survive it as well. That is established expert supported science.

Movies also portray very small lasers as having tremendous power to cut thick metal doors. Is that really possible? Lasers only emit a small percentage of the power necessary to produce and maintain the laser beam. Small handheld lasers such as a laser pointer have very low power and can do very little damage unless they are pointed into the eyes. Even then the damage may only be temporary. I trained students on a bigger 5-watt laser that could burn the skin and maybe over time burn a mark on a painted wall. The beam came from a laser head weighing about 80 pounds and was supplied with power from 3-phase 50 amp per phase 240-volt power supply also weighing in excess of 80 pounds. That laser was water cooled. Even with that much power, that laser would never be able to cut through a heavy metal door. Movies like Star Trek, Star Wars, James Bond, etc. have the characters cutting through very thick metal doors with laser emanating from small hand-held devices or even a wristwatch. The movies also typically use a red laser. Red lasers are among the least powerful colors for a laser. I blocked smaller red lasers routinely with my hand when multiple lasers were aligned. I would not do it with a blue or ultraviolet laser because it would burn my hand. Movie stars, though, can do almost anything with a red laser.

There are other illustrations but let's not spoil the enjoyment of these movies. The point is should we raise these story tellers to the level of "experts" and their stories as facts? Storytellers are not just in Hollywood. Almost anyone can tell a story. News people do so every day. Politicians do it. We are bombarded with storytelling ads. Everyone does it at some point. Can we rely, however, that every storyteller has the facts right, and tells the truth? Should we believe every story and elevate every storyteller to the level of "Expert"?

One last thing, should we pass on stories because we like them without checking the facts? Some things sound good, even right but may not be correct. Something does **NOT** become true just because a lot of people say it is so.

See if these points make sense:

1. It takes time and study and an intimate involvement with a subject to become an expert.
2. Those who are experts are only considered experts in a very narrow field of study.
3. Experts may have little or no knowledge outside of their expertise.
4. There may be no human experts on some subjects.
5. Should we grant expert status based on emotion or because people are good story tellers?
6. Should we pass on unverified stories?

CHAPTER 2
WORLDVIEWS

A *World View* by definition is a particular philosophy of life or conception of the world. Everyone has one but not everyone expresses it. Some people simply parrot the principles told to them by people who influenced their lives. They may not even think deeply about it, but it comes out when people say:

That is not right.
That is not fair.
What is my purpose?
Etc.

There a website called Worldviewu.org that listed some questions that a world view tries to answer:

1. How did I get here?
2. Why are we here?
3. Where are we going?
4. Who is in charge?
5. What is true?
6. What is right and what is wrong?

The site lists many examples of world views. The answer given for the first question is typically:

1. We evolved over time totally without any divine intervention.
2. God created everything.
3. God and naturalistic evolution produced everything.

The starting point of a world view, centers around what we believe is true about God. The atheist believes there is no God. Judaism, Christianity, Islam, etc. believe there is a God. Others on the world view list try to integrate God and chance evolution. The answer we choose for the first question often dictates how we will answer the others. Those who do not believe there is a God believe that time and chance produced life. They view the world as a struggle of life and death with no purpose, only the strongest in charge, no absolute truth, and no absolute right or wrong. Those that believe in God might say that God is in charge, that we all have a purpose, that He provides absolute truth and therefore there is absolute right and wrong.

Are there any human experts when it comes to the study of origins? Can we study those past events? If evolution is true and the world has now been in existence for the millions and billions of years claimed by the evolutionist, then the time frames are excessive. Unless you have a time machine that can go back in time and view the change of one species into another, there is no way to study the process. If you cannot study evolution, then how can anyone become an expert in it? Are those promoting evolution just storytellers? Should a story simply be accepted as fact when it cannot be proven? The scientists telling the evolution story are often granted expert status, simply because they have earned high degrees in science.

Does expertise in one narrow area make someone an expert in a completely different area?

To be fair here, those that believe that God exists and that He created everything are also telling a story.

In the beginning God created the heavens and the earth. (Gen 1:1)

None of us can verify that story either and for the same reason as the evolution story. We cannot go back in time and observe God creating everything. It should be noted though, if God did it, He was there and He would be an expert! Do we believe in the possible expert, God, or do we believe in storytellers that can never be experts in our origins?

Many believe the Biblical account is the correct story. You may disagree and that is your right. If the evolution story cannot be defended logically or scientifically, should it be accepted as fact? There is incredible complexity of even the simplest forms of life. Could all of that really happen by chance?

Suppose for the moment you were to discover a diamond ring in the sand on a beach. What would be your first thought as to how it got there? Most people would say that someone lost the ring. If you picked up a rounded pebble on the beach and asked the same question, would anyone say, "that someone lost the pebble". What is the difference? The diamond ring exhibits an incredible amount of design that could not simply be the result of the action of the waves and wind beating on the sandy shore. Waves and wind, on the other hand, could easily account for the rounding of the pebble. The difference is design. The diamond ring exhibits a careful intelligent design, the rounded pebble does not.

Our knowledge of even the simplest form of life has increased dramatically in the last 100 years to the point that we can no longer regard the "simple" cell as simple. It is incredibly complex. If you were to attempt to build one from scratch, what would you need?

Here is a list:

1. A shell to hold all the parts.
2. Portals through the shell that would open for "food" but remain closed for harmful materials.
3. Some form of locomotion (cilia, a flagellum, etc.)
4. A decomposition site in the cell to break down raw materials.
5. A construction site to build needed molecules (proteins, nucleic acids, etc.)
6. A mechanism to fold a molecule into its proper shape.
7. A transportation system to carry all of these materials within the cell and remove waste.
8. A DNA molecule in the nucleus of the cell to control and monitor everything.

Doesn't this sound like a modern manufacturing plant on a microscopic level? Are these simple cells the result of intelligent design not random chance?

One more point, in actual living cells, none of the parts can exist long by themselves and the living cell cannot exist long without its parts. It all had to come together quickly to exist.

The Bible tells us:

For the wrath of God is revealed from heaven against all ungodliness and unrighteousness of men, who suppress the truth in unrighteousness, because what may be known of God is manifest in them, for God has shown it to them. For since the creation of the world His invisible attributes are clearly seen, being understood by the things that are made, even His eternal power and Godhead, so that they are without excuse, (Romans 1:18-20)

Isn't the Bible simply saying that if you study the world, you will see the evidence for God? There are those who disagree. They are mentioned in the Bible in Psalm 14:1. Romans chapter one beginning in verse 18 describes the inevitable results of such thinking. Read it for yourselves. Does it sound like our world today?

If this is true, isn't the most reasonable defensible world view puts God at its center? Many are also convinced that the Bible is the best source of information about God, truth, man, and our interaction with God. You are free to disagree. You have the right to your opinion too, but no one can claim to be experts on origins.

DAVID P. MCINTYRE

CHAPTER 3
THE BIBLICAL VIEWPOINT

God Centered

The Biblical viewpoint is that everything begins with God. He is the Creator.

In the beginning God created the heavens and the earth. (Genesis 1:1)

To those who doubt that He made it, He says:

Where were you when I laid the foundations of the earth? Tell me if you have understanding. (Job 38:4)

Ecclesiastes tells us:

Remember now your Creator in the days of your youth, (Ecclesiastes 12:1a)

The New Testament also refers to God as the Creator.

In the beginning was the Word, and the Word was with God, and the Word was God. He was in the beginning with God. All things were made through Him, and without Him nothing was made that was made. (John 1:1-3)

The first book of the Bible goes on to say all the other things that God created, light, darkness, plants, living things, sun, moon, stars, and finally man. If all of that is true, then everything belongs to God. If we claim to own any of it, we are all squatters and claim jumpers! If He is the Creator, then He is deserving of respect, praise, glory, and worship. It would also explain God's views on things.

Race

The Bible viewpoint is that there is only one Race, The Human Race.

> *Then God said "Let Us make man in Our image, according to Our likeness; let them have dominion over the fish of the sea, over the birds of the air, and over the cattle, over all the earth and over every creeping thing that creeps on the earth." (Gen 1:26)*

The Bible does not specify characteristics of man. He did build variety into the DNA so that future offspring would not all look exactly alike. Look at the variety He created in other living things. Some may be tall, others short. Eye color may be different. Hair color and texture may be different. Some have much better tans than others. No one type is better than another. Should we answer the form question alluding to race, with words "Human Race"? Are those using the term "racist" really just trying to pick a fight with their fellow human beings? If the Bible is correct, then we are all related all the way back to Adam and Eve. Are we just fighting with our relatives like the "Hatfield's and McCoy's". Does that really honor God?

If you pick up a tube of blood and look at it, there is no way that anyone can tell from whom it came. They all look the same. If an organ is donated for transplant, again there is no way to visually determine the physical characteristics of the donor.

There are T-shirts with the slogan: "Black Lives Matter". Black lives do matter. The life of the man being kicked and beaten on television on Martin Luther King's Day matters. The store owner's life whose shop was damaged by a man throwing a brick through the shop window during a riot matters. The policeman's life who was shot and killed while sitting in his police car matters. The people wounded or killed by an angry gunman matter. It isn't just black lives; it is all lives. When our fellow human beings are mistreated, it matters; it does not justify, though, mistreating others.

While there is only one Human Race, there are different cultures, traditions, music, etc. We do not all have the same likes, but we can all respect and treat each other well. We can enjoy different cultures, cuisines, and music. In every group, we can find people we like to be around and people we would prefer not to be around. It has nothing to do with their physical characteristics; it has everything to do with how they personally conduct themselves. Would you like to be around people, for example, who are loud, angry, constantly using the "F-word"? Are you comfortable being around people who drink way too much and push everyone else to drink like they do? Do you like bullies? Are you comfortable in the presence of those who are continually bickering and complaining? Nothing seems to please them.

Sex

Notice also that in Genesis 1:26, that He created just two sexes, male and female.

So, God created man in His own image; in the image of God, He created him; male and female He created them. (Genesis 1:26-27)

He even hardwired it into the DNA. Every male has a X and a Y chromosome, and every female has just two X chromosomes. Those chromosomes make a difference in the structure and sex organs of the two individuals. If an individual dies and someone were to dig up their bones, the examiner would easily identify whether they were male or female by their bone structure. The sex organs complement each other. The male Y chromosome also generates other physical characteristics. Males tend to be overall stronger than the females. That is why female (XX) athletes are objecting to competing against those who have the X and Y chromosome where strength is a primary factor. Is it really fair competition?

You can believe in the anything goes mentality prevalent in the world today. From that viewpoint, you can participate in alternate lifestyles, try to change your sex, or even think of yourself as an animal of some sort. Are there any limits to that viewpoint? If God exists and the Bible is true though, then those making such choices will have the opportunity to explain their choice to God. In fact, the Bible says we all will.

And as it is appointed for men to die once, but after this the judgement, (Heb 9:27)

Our grandson asked me a question as to how I would interact with someone with a different sex view. Rather than just denounce the alternative viewpoint, I told him a story about a friend of mine to illustrate my response. The friend was a fishing buddy. I thoroughly enjoyed fishing with him and for years he and I would go on another friend's boat for a week of fishing in the Bahamas. Every time we went, my friend would put 7 cases of beer, 24 cans per case, in the hold of the boat. There would be one case for every day we would be in the Bahamas. He would then drink beer at the rate of about three cans every hour we fished. The owner of the boat and I did not approve of the drinking habit. Our mutual friend knew it, but he also knew we loved and cared about him. We all thoroughly enjoyed each other's company. We did not feel we had the right to dictate his choices. Do we, however, have to agree with those choices? Do those making alternative choices have the right to demand that we agree?

The Founding Fathers knew they could not force God and the Bible on others. They believed in persuasion not coercion. If everyone is forced to accept the latest viewpoints, then where is the freedom of speech and religion so cherished by those founders?

Marriage

The Bible tells us that the first marriage was performed by God between Adam and Eve.

> And the LORD said, "It is not good that man should be alone; I will make a helper comparable to him." (Genesis 2:18)

> And the LORD God caused a deep sleep to fall on Adam, and he slept; and He took one of his ribs and closed up the flesh in its place. Then the rib which the LORD God had taken from man

He made into a woman, and He brought her to the man. And Adam said:

"This is now bone of my bones and flesh of my flesh; She shall be called Woman because she was taken out of man."

Therefore, a man shall leave his father and mother and be joined to his wife, and they shall become one flesh. And they were both naked, the man and his wife, and they were not ashamed. (Genesis 2:21-25)

This first marriage set the standard for all marriages to follow. It was to be between one male and one female. They were to become one flesh. They were to leave their family and form a new family unit. Divorce, while later allowed, was not the original intent. Divorce tears the "flesh" union. They also need not to be ashamed of enjoying each other's bodies, but later references make it clear, especially in the Ten Commandments (Exodus 20) that adultery was not allowed.

Marriage was not primarily for pleasure although it is pleasurable. It was for procreation and protection of children. The implication in Genesis 2:24 is that there would be a father and a mother left behind when forming the new marriage. Are most of our problems with our youths today the result of a tearing of the "flesh" where one parent separates from the other or does not fulfill the father or mother roles well? Doesn't every child long to know and be loved by both their father and their mother? Doesn't the loss of either one hurt them? I am the oldest of three brothers. We lost our mother to cancer when I was four and a half years old. All of us were affected by the loss. My brother Dennis wrote a book entitled *Legacy of Love* in which he expressed his feelings as a cry to be loved. Even though she has been gone for over seventy years, I still miss my mother. I would give almost anything to have another day with her, another hour.

Being a parent is an incredible responsibility. Parents must meet their children's needs. They are also to protect, teach and guide that precious life. They need protection especially in the early years because they have no idea what can hurt them. They will put anything in their mouth. Pills, poison, pesticides, almost anything they can reach is fair game for the taste test. They will touch everything, the knife that falls on the floor, the dog poop (that will also likely succumb to the taste test as well), a hot stove. They do not understand yet what is safe and what can harm them. They are simply discovering their world. If the parent is not vigilant that child could hurt or even kill themselves. How many children have died drowning in a pool because parents were not watchful.

Those same children also learn to trust those parents. They believe everything they are told whether it is true or not. Early on, they have no way to discern fact from falsehood. Isn't it extremely important then that parent's control and filter what is being taught to them? Children have been used to kill, steal, and participate in all kinds of sexual perversions following some pied piper adult they trusted. The Biblical principle is that the parents are to teach their children Biblical truth (Deut 4:9). If they are not taught truth, how else can they discern right from wrong?

Parents also need to discipline children. The Bible equates discipline with love.

He who spares the rod hates his son, but he who loves him disciplines him promptly. (Prov 13:24)

How else do they learn right behavior versus wrong behavior and the consequences? It is the parents that must guide their child into becoming a responsible citizen of society. It is a daunting task. Because it is, is it right for people to claim they are a mom or a dad simply because they are egg or sperm donors?

Single parenting a child is a tremendous burden on the parent doing the job. They all need help at times because a female has difficulty fulfilling the father role and a male the mother role. They are not designed for it. Thankfully there are institutions that help single mothers. There need to be a lot more. My brothers and I are very thankful that after our mother died, we did experience a father and mother foster family to help Dad. They raised their own children and then shared love and discipline with us. I wonder what might have happened to us if God had not provided that experience. What trouble might we have gotten into expressing our anger and frustration. A marriage between a man and a woman can fulfill by themselves the role of procreation and protection of children. Doesn't a same sex union require a third party for procreation? If a third-party leaves, will the child be affected as we were by the loss?

You have the right to disagree. However, the statistics seem to show a correlation between the breakup of traditional families and the increase in the crime rate. If this nation really wants to reduce that rate, shouldn't we consider restoring, supporting, and honoring the traditional Biblical marriage? There can be agreements for financial and other considerations and still uphold traditional marriage.

The Fetus

The Biblical viewpoint of the fetus in the womb is that from the very start it is a child! Read Psalm 139.

For You formed my inward parts; You covered me in my mother's womb. I will praise You for I am fearfully and wonderfully made; marvelous are Your works, and that my soul knows very well. My frame was not hidden from You, when I was made in secret, and skillfully wrought in the lowest parts of the earth. Your eyes saw my substance being yet unformed, and in Your book they all were written, the days fashioned for me, when as yet there were none of them. (Psalm 139:13-16)

That Bible statement was way ahead of its time. It was less than 100 years ago that scientists discovered DNA molecules. We now know that that molecule contains the blueprint to build every part of the child. There are people who can read blueprints of a building and from them envision what the building will look like when finished. They create artist renditions of those visions. The Bible is telling us that God could read that blueprint and envision exactly how we would look right down to the smallest detail. We also know now that that blueprint remains the same from the time, we were just a single cell in the womb to the end of our lives. It never changes. The courts now rely on DNA tests to prove guilt or innocence, establish paternity, determine ancestry, and so forth. Isn't The Bible indicating that the fetus is a human being right from conception?

There are those who claim that a woman has the right to do anything she wants with her body. I would agree. She can change her hips, fatten her lips, lift her face, and pack things in any place. I might not agree that it improves anything, but I will agree that she has the right to do it. Those same people may also say that the fetus is just part of the woman's body and therefore she has the right to abort it if she chooses. They make the claim in nice sounding words like "it is a difficult decision, but the woman should make the choice". The one question that is totally ignored, though: "Is the fetus just part of her body?" Any woman can attempt to make the case that it is by just comparing her DNA to the DNA of the fetus. If it matches exactly, she has made her case and all disagreement disappears. If it does not, however, and the fetus DNA is human, then the opposite is true. The fetus is a separate human being. It is not her body! True, it is not fully developed, but it is following the human DNA blueprint to make another human being. The point of fact is that it will not be fully developed for another 18 or more years after the fetus has left the womb. Now we must come to grips with the fact she has a separate human being inside her. According to our laws, no one has the right to take the life of another human being. If a man attacks a woman and she loses the fetus inside her, he can be charged with murder or at least manslaughter. The real question then is whether the woman should be granted the special right to take the life of the fetus. If the fetus is a separate human being, shouldn't it be granted all rights that all the rest of us enjoy by the Constitution and the Bill of Rights including Life Liberty and the pursuit of happiness?

Every time an abortion is performed, with rare exceptions, the fetus dies. Since the Biblical view appears to be that the fetus is a child, a child is being killed. Over 60 million fetuses have been killed since the Roe Vs Wade Supreme Court decision. The Bible has many stories in the Old Testament of nations being destroyed by God as a result of killing their children. What must God think of us for killing our children?

The Rules

I think most people have heard of the Ten Commandments. Can you name all ten? Most people will be able to list some of them, maybe even the majority of them, but all ten will likely be more of a challenge. They are located in Exodus 20:2-17 and again in Deuteronomy 5:6-21. Biblically, they are God's commandments. If we do not know what they are, how can we keep them? Depictions of Moses and the Ten Commandments are found in the Supreme Court and many state court buildings. I found an interesting quote from an essay that came up online by Gary Demar.

> *State courtrooms and government buildings across our land have housed similar displays for decades without any legal challenge. "In fact, the Ten Commandments are more easily found in America's government buildings than in her religious buildings, thus demonstrating the understanding by generations of Americans from coast to coast that the Ten Commandments formed the basis of America's civil laws."*[1]

Not only are these Commandments Biblical, but they were also well respected by the Founding Fathers. They likely formed the basis for our laws. They are our heritage.

The first four relate to our relationship with God. The Bible says that God created all things. It also says in many passages that He is the only God and there is no other God (examples: Isaiah 44:6, 8;

---

[1] Gary Demar, The Ten Commandments and the Supreme Court, The American Vision, November 21, 2006.

45:5,6,21; 47:10). The first three make perfect sense if you imagine for a moment you are standing beside God and watching how man on earth interacts with Him.

I.   Do not have any other Gods before me.

II.   Do not make any idols.

III. Do not take the name of the LORD God in vain.

Would God take it well to be ignored? Is the Atheist placing himself as the ultimate authority and not God? The Bible indicates that God will have the last word on that issue. Idols can be anything that gets between us and God. That can be money, fame, fortune, other people, etc. Idols keep us from acknowledging and worshipping the Creator. Would God take it well to have His or His Son's name used as swear words? Everyone that has spoken the name of Jesus Christ in anger, spoken the words represented by the letters GD, is guilty of violating number three. The Bible indicates that this is God's world, and He is deserving of worship, praise, and obedience.

The fourth commandment is as much for man as for God.

IV.   Keep the Sabbath

First, we are to worship Him and Him only. Second, the seven-day week does not have any celestial basis like years (time for earth to travel around the sun), months (based on the motion of the moon), or days (the time for one rotation of the earth). It is solely based on the Biblical account of Creation in which God created everything in six days and then **rested** on the seventh. He set the example of resting one day in seven. We are to do the same. We are to work, but no one is to be a workaholic with no periodic rest.

All the rest of the Commandments show us how we are to relate to our fellow man. They make perfect sense when we view them from the receiving end, that is others doing to us. Here is the list.

V.   Honor your mother and father.

VI.   Do not murder.

VII.   Do not commit adultery.

VIII.   Do not steal.

IX.   Do not lie.

X.   Do not covet (or be jealous).

What parent does not want their children to honor and obey them? Who wants to be murdered by someone around them? What wife or husband is OK with their spouse cheating on them? How many of you enjoy having your things stolen, people lie to you, or have someone be jealous of what you have? All of these things lead to conflict. Conflict leads to anger, riots, people getting hurt, and maybe even war. God was trying to protect us!

The last six and maybe even the last seven might even be acceptable to the Atheist. The real reason they want to remove the Ten Commandments from government buildings is because they want to impose their godless religion on everyone else. An atheist on TV once said that he wanted "freedom from religion". I thought about his statement, and I think I agree with him. He does not want God and the Bible forced on him. I do not want his atheistic religion forced on me.

The Founding Fathers did not want a "state" religion, but clearly revered God and the Bible. You are free to believe whatever you wish. In this book I am expressing facts about the Founding Fathers and sometimes my personal beliefs. I hope you will allow me to express those beliefs whether you agree with them or not. I thank you ahead of time if you do. Many believe this country has been blessed more than any other country in the world because our Founding Fathers based our foundation on God and the Bible. Would removing God or references to Him mean that He will remove His protection from us? Would that also mean the downfall of our nation?

Those that do not want to abide by the rules are also setting an example for how others are to treat them. How can a person who does not honor his parents expect his children to honor him? A killer will worry that others will kill him or her. If people steal, how can they claim that it is not right to steal from them? The Biblical principle is that you reap what you sow (Galatians 6:7).

Man

Right from the start, the Bible shows us that while man was made in God's image (Genesis 1:26, 27), God could not trust man to keep the rules. Long before the Ten Commandments, Adam and Eve were given one simple commandment, do not eat of the tree of the knowledge of good and evil (Genesis 2:17). Genesis 2 tells us that God planted a gorgeous garden for Adam and Eve and that they could eat freely from the trees in that garden (Genesis 2:16) except for one. He just kept one out of maybe thousands or even millions of others for Himself. They could not keep the commandment. Genesis 3 tells the story of their fall and God's punishment banning them from the garden. Adam and Eve had sinned against God. The Garden of Eden was God's. God then removed Adam and Eve from the Garden. God demonstrated even back then that sin cannot be allowed in God's place whether the Garden of Eden or Heaven. The earth was cursed and that would now be their home.

There are those that say that man is basically good and that circumstances make him bad. The Bible does not agree. Man has to be trained and disciplined to follow the rules and become a functioning citizen in society. Babies learn very quickly how to manipulate parents. Many babies have cried not because they are hungry, need changing, or have some other need but solely because of a want. They want attention and control. If they do not get what they want, they act worse. Almost every parent has experienced the "terrible twos" when children escalate to temper tantrums to get their way.

It carries over to grownups too. There was a Christian radio program in which the male announcer admitted that occasionally he gets mad and hollers a bit. One of the lady announcers told him he was having a "Mantrum", a male temper tantrum. What an inciteful label! I have been guilty too. Maybe even women are guilty as well. The news is often full of anger and riots. Are we seeing two-year-old temper tantrums in fully grown men and women?

The Bible tells us that everybody like Adam and Eve have or will sin.

> *The LORD looks down from heaven upon the children of men, to see if there are any who understand, who seek God. They have all turned aside, they have together become corrupt; there is none who does good, no, not one. (Psalm 14:2,3)*

> *For all have sinned and fall short of the glory of God. (Romans 3:23)*

What do we get for that sin?

For the wages of sin is death,.. (Romans 6:23a)

Therefore, just as through one man sin entered the world, and death by sin, and thus death spread to all men, because all sinned. (Romans 5:12)

We hear ads all the time telling us to "get all that you deserve", "Have it your way", and "You deserve it". If the Bible is true and we are sinners before a Holy God, do we really want to get what we deserve? Thank God that is not the end of the Bible story. God created man in His image with the free will to choose right or wrong. When man sinned, he hinted all the way back in Genesis 3:15 that He had a plan through the seed of woman to redeem man. If man could not keep the rules than God would become a man and keep the rules for him.

In the beginning was the Word and the Word was with God. And the Word was God. (John 1:1)

And the Word became flesh and dwelt among us, and we beheld His glory, the glory as of the only begotten of the Father, full of grace and truth. (John 1:14)

Do not think that I came to destroy the Law or the Prophets. I did not Come to destroy but to fulfill. (Matthew 5:17)

Since breaking the rules brings death, Jesus had to die to pay the penalty for our sin.

But God demonstrates His own love toward us, in that while we were yet sinners, Christ died for us. (Romans 5:8)

Adam and Eve needed to just trust in God about the tree of the knowledge of good and evil. Essentially, God is wooing us today to do the same thing by putting our faith and trust in Jesus.

For God so loved the world that He gave His only begotten Son, that whoever believes in Him should not perish but have everlasting life. (John 3:16)

Mankind is being given a second chance. Do we really want to blow it again as Adam and Eve did?

You may disagree. If the Bible is true, though, where will you go when this life is over?

Work

God sets the example in the very first chapter in Genesis; He worked six days to create everything. He expects man to work too. Work is not worrisome or a burden. It gives purpose. It is a source of pride. We identify with our chosen vocation as a part of who we are. It is a good thing. Shouldn't everyone who is able to work, work and pay their own way? Those who refuse are like leeches sucking the "blood" out of the nation. God also has something to say about those who refuse to work. The Apostle Paul seemed to equate those who were disorderly and busybodies with those that would not work.

But we command you, brethren, in the name of our Lord Jesus Christ, that you withdraw from every brother who walks disorderly and not according to the traditions which he received from us, For you yourselves know how you ought to follow us, for we were not disorderly among you; nor did we eat anyone's bread free of charge, but worked with labor and toil night and day, that we might not be a burden to any of you, not because we do not have authority, but to make ourselves an example of how you should follow us. For even when we were with you, we commanded you this: if anyone will not work, neither shall he eat. For we hear that there are some who walk among you in a disorderly manner, not working at all, but are busybodies. (2 Thessalonians 3:6-11)

Many believe in helping neighbors in times of distress or crisis. Many, especially Christians will give to those needs, sending food, clothing, and needed supplies to disaster victims. We may be reluctant, though, to give to a beggar on the street because we do not know if they really are in distress, or they just want money for drugs or alcohol.

Do giveaways provide work, or do they encourage people not to work? Why should our nation go into greater debt to support those who will not work? It is not uncommon to find businesses hiring and not able to find workers.

Debt

Money manager experts tell us that we need to work to get out of debt as quickly as we can.

The rich rules over the poor and the borrower is servant to the lender. (Proverbs 22:7)

The word translated servant in that verse essentially means in bondage like a slave. Now the ideal would be that we save up the money for things and then buy them when we have enough. Obviously, this is not an ideal world so lenders will lend money to buy things.

Keep in mind though, they are doing so to make money. Nothing is free. It always costs someone something. If the lender is reputable and the interest rate is not too outrageous, we all justify borrowing to pay for big items like a house or a car. The same principle applies though, pay off the debt as quickly as possible. Shouldn't the goal for everyone be that we eventually reach a point where we are debt free and live that way from then on? Isn't getting out of debt common sense?

Shouldn't our government get out of debt as well and for the same reason? Americans do not realize that debt makes us servants (literally slaves) to the lender. If we cannot pay our debts, our homes, our cars, or whatever we have put up as collateral can be confiscated. What is the collateral for public debt? If we have a lot of debt and the creditors call in the loans, we are in big trouble. What would happen if our nation's creditors were to call in the national debt loans? Wouldn't our nation also be in really serious trouble? We cannot live individually beyond our means indefinitely. Somehow our government seems to think they can. Is this really true or will there be a reckoning someday?

There is another aspect of debt which reduces the net amount of money we have to spend, interest. The interest needs to be paid first. It is no different with our government. The interest has to be paid. If it is not, our credit rating suffers, and we cannot borrow any more money. The current national debt is 31.1 trillion dollars.[2] Current interest rates are rising. We just applied for an equity loan on our house and was quoted at 5.75 %. If the government had to pay that kind of interest on the national debt, it would amount to almost 1.8

---

[2] " Impact, Key Drivers, Current US Debt", Investopedia, October 21, 2022.

trillion dollars in just interest! To put this in perspective, I looked up the federal budget for 2022. It was 6.011 trillion dollars.[3] That comes out to almost 30 % of the budget! It is even worse than that, because the government is taking in far less than 6.011 trillion dollars. If they want to meet the budget, they will have to borrow more money which increases the interest payment even further. Our government spending is spiraling out of control and yet government leaders are bent on giving away money they do not have. If we did this, our credit rating would plumet and we would not be able to borrow any more money. We would be forced to live within our means after all interest is paid. If the government has to do this, they will have to raise taxes by huge amounts or cut services to all of us. The consequences will be horrendous. The great depression of 1929 might be considered mild in comparison. Is living on credit really a good idea?

Money managers will also tell you to save money in two basic accounts, a long-term, and short-term. The long-term account will eventually be used to provide money when a person is no longer able to work. The short-term account is used for emergencies so that the person does not have to go deeper in debt. Many years ago, someone shared these simple ideas with me. My wife and I worked to pay off our mortgage and now we own our home. We added money and increased the amount over the years in a 401 K plan. We now have income in our older years. Our house air conditioner needed to be replaced. We had the money in a short-term account. It works! We are no longer servants to lenders.

---

[3] Kimberly Armadeo, "Us Federal Budget Breakdown", The Balance, June 24, 2022.

CHAPTER 4
ONE NATION UNDER GOD

The Founding Fathers, God, and the Bible

Our nation's Founding Fathers had a reverence for God and the Bible. Consider the opening statements in the Declaration of Independence:

> When in the Course of human events, it becomes necessary for one people to dissolve the political bands which have connected them with another, and to assume among the powers of the earth, the separate and equal station to which the **Laws of Nature and of Nature's God** entitle them, a decent respect to the opinions of mankind requires that they should declare the causes which impel them to the separation.

> We hold these truths to be self-evident, that all men are created equal, that they are **endowed by their Creator** with certain unalienable Rights, that among these are Life, Liberty, and the pursuit of Happiness.

While the Constitution does not reference God or the divine, but every state constitution does so at least once. Beginning with George Washington and every president afterwards ended the oath of office with the words "So help me God". The Bible was present in administering the first presidential oath and in all subsequent oaths. Historians claimed Washington said at his inaugural:

> *"We ought to be no less persuaded that the propitious smiles of heaven can never be expected on a nation that disregards the eternal rules of order and the right which heaven itself has ordained."* [4]

Currently, even our money says, "In God We Trust".

Those Founding Fathers viewed God as the Creator. As such, He owns the entire creation. Man, then, is at best the manager of God's creation but not the owner. God was also deserving of worship. To worship properly, though, man needed to understand God, His purpose, His desires, and how best to interact with Him. The Founding Fathers felt that the Bible was the best source of information to achieve those goals.

Prior to the colonization of America, King James of England commissioned the translation of the Old Testament and the New Testament from the original languages into English. The completed Bible was published in 1611. It became the official Bible of the official Church of England. There were problems, though, but not with the Bible. A group of Christians wanted to study the Bible on their own. They found the strict ceremonial worship and control by the King of England were at odds with the teachings of the Bible. At first, they tried to purify the church and became known as Puritans. When they were unsuccessful, they decided to leave England for America. 102 of them led by William Bradford, boarded the Mayflower, and

---

[4] Tom Hughes, America Dedicated to God, Alliance For Religious Freedom.

set sail along with 30 crewmen for the new world. It took 66 days to cross the Atlantic. When they stepped out on land, Indians, the Native Americans, attacked them. They had to reboard and sailed another three weeks to find a better landing site. They finally landed at Plymouth Rock near Cape Cod. It was December, the beginning of winter. Almost half of them died in the brutal winter that followed. Interestingly another Native American named Squanto ended up saving them. You can get online and see artwork depicting the first Thanksgiving with Squanto. William Bradford later alluded to Romans 8:28 in his diary.[5]

And we know that all things work together for good to those who love God, to those who are the called according to His purpose. (Romans 8:28)

The new arrivals to the Americas brought the King James Bible with them. Later, there was conflict with England. Since England owned the copyright for the King James Bible, it became difficult to obtain them, Congress authorized Robert Aiken to print the King James Bible in America. He did so in 1782. His version became known as the "Bible of the Revolution".[6]

The point here is that our Founding Fathers believed in God and the Bible. Rather than separating the Bible from public exposure, they integrated it into the public arena.

Religion

The Founding Fathers also appeared to not want to reproduce the mistake that England and other countries made in designating

[5] The Mayflower Story, 1620-2020 Mayflower 400, Stories of the Mayflower
[6] The KJV in Early America, Cedarville University, Biblical Heritage Gallery, The King James Bible

a particular belief as the state church. There is no reference in the original Constitution to a "Church of the United States". They did, however, say within Article 6 that:

> *"..no religious test shall ever be required as a Qualification to any office or public trust under the United States."*

Also, in the Bill of Rights the First Amendment states.

> *Congress shall make no law respecting an establishment of religion or prohibiting the free exercise thereof; or abridging the freedom of speech, or of the press; or the right of people peacefully to assemble, and to petition the Government for a redress of grievances.*

I think they realized that everyone has a world view and essentially that view involves a belief system. That is who we are. We bring that system with us. It establishes how we think and view the world around us. Any attempt to limit it is a little like asking someone to leave their right arm outside whenever you enter a government establishment.

How we exercise that belief system and demonstrate it establishes our religious beliefs. People who believe in God, flesh out that belief in religious practices. The Atheist is also doing the same thing when he states, "there is no God". In order to claim the statement is absolutely true, he would have to be able to go everywhere in all the dimensions of the universe simultaneously to determine there is no God anywhere. No person except God can do that! The Atheist is expressing his belief, not an established fact. Those who believe in God and the Atheist will both reflect their belief in their practices and point of view. The Atheist is as much religious as anyone else.

Do either the believer in God or the Atheist have the right to force their belief on anyone else?

Since about the 1960's, there has been a continuous push to remove all references to God out of our state institutions, particularly our public schools. Would the Founding Fathers approve? Wouldn't they accuse The Government of trying to establish a state religion, Atheism? Many, like the Puritans, left England precisely because England did exactly that through the Church of England. King James told people what to believe through that church. Today, are we trying to do the same thing in the United States? Isn't this a violation of our rights, and should the Government be petitioned to redress it? Should people be forced to silence their faith? If anyone initiates prayer in public schools, why not let them. Others do not have to agree but should be respectful and quiet. If some wish to study the Bible in schools, why not let them. No one should be forced to participate. Years ago, students were allowed to attend religious education classes in public schools. No one was forced to attend. Why should anyone to be upset about it now? It was simply an elective option.

By pushing all references to God and the Bible out of the public institutions, is the government "Separating Church and State" or establishing the state religion of Atheism to the exclusion of all others? Science classes teach evolution as an established fact. Many scientists with earned higher degrees disagree. There are a number of books expressing that viewpoint. Can anyone be an expert on origins if it cannot be studied? Can scientists go back in time and observe the process of changing one form of life into a completely different one (fish to amphibian, amphibian to reptile, reptile to bird, etc.) to test the validity of evolution? If the answer is no, can it really even be called a theory? A theory is a hypothesis (a story) that has undergone rigorous observation and testing. If the story appears to be true in each test, it is elevated to the level of theory. If it cannot pass the tests, it is changed until it can pass the tests or discarded as just another story. If you cannot study origins, how can there be any experts? The only possible expert is God.

Hitler used the concept of evolution to justify the extermination of the Jewish population. He thought of himself and the Arian people as more evolved and justified Jewish extermination based on "survival of the fittest". Are we covertly teaching racism in public schools under the guise of science? Add to that the attempts to infiltrate schools with the Critical Race Theory (CRT) attributed to the Atheist Karl Marx, are schools trying to make everyone racist?

Eliminate the idea there is an absolute right or wrong, then anything someone can conjure up may be taught as Ok, even normal. Those who believe in God and the Bible would disagree. They feel there is an absolute right and wrong. Shouldn't parents be involved in the decision of what is taught?

Education

The Bible tells us that children are a gift from God and that parents are to nurture and teach them in ways of the Lord. Education in early America was largely the responsibility of parents. They spent time teaching their children how to read, write, and maybe some math. They passed on history. Their textbook, you guessed it, the Bible. Many just used the same Kings James Bible they brought with them to the new world. They felt it was important that their children learn to read so they could read the Bible for themselves. It was only later that when some parents were not able or did not wish to teach their children that public schools began to appear. It was important to the Founding Fathers that children learn to read, write, do math, and know their history so they could take their place in society. Those who do not have such skills are handicapped. Even then, though, teachers did not teach subjects contrary to the parents' wishes.

It was interesting that as far back as 1647, Massachusetts passed what became known as the "ye old deluder, Satan" act. It required that all towns of 50 or more families hire teachers to instruct the children in reading and writing. They wanted to ensure that children could read the Bible for themselves. They wanted those children to discern truth and not be led astray by "Satan's charismatic storytellers". The name was derived from the law's preamble:

"It being one chief project of that old deluder, Satan, to keep men from the knowledge of the Scriptures,"[7]

Later, other colonies followed Massachusetts' example.

Even the most widely used textbook reader, **The New England Primer,** was based on the Bible. It was used until well into the 19th century.

---

[7] Massachusetts School Laws, Text of the Massachusetts General School Law of 1647, Wikipedia.

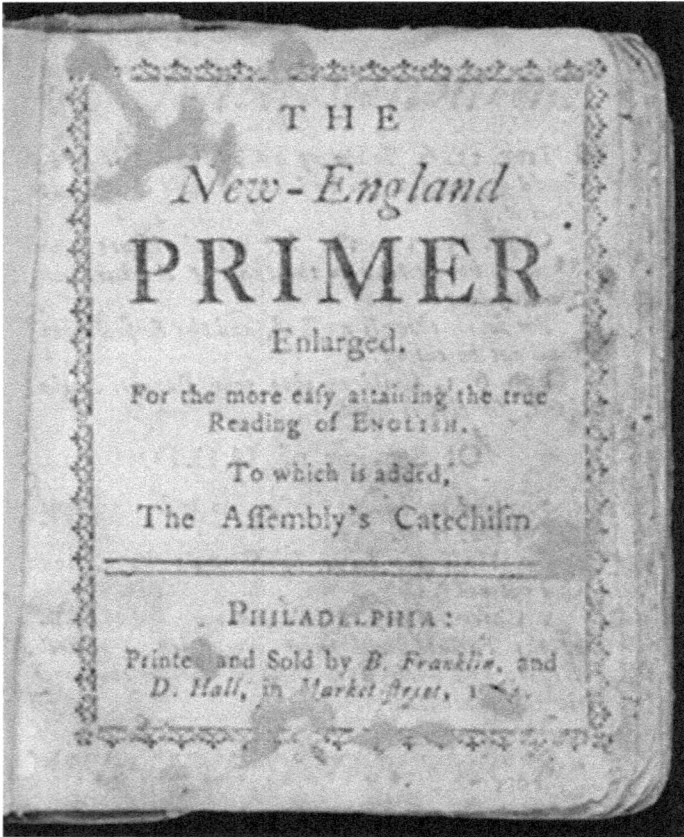

If you look at the cover, you will see that it was printed and sold by Benjamin Franklin. Does that name ring a bell? References to the Bible appeared throughout the reader. According to Wikipedia[8] the following diagrams are examples.

In Adam's fall
We sinned all.

Thy life to mend,
This Book attend.

The Cat doth play,
And after slay.

A Dog will bite
A thief at night.

An Eagle's flight
Is out of sight

The idle Fool
Is whipt at school.

As runs the Glass,
Man's life doth pass.

My Book and Heart
Shall never part.

Job feels the rod,
And blesses God.

Proud Korah's troops
Were swallowed up.

The Lion bold
The lamb doth hold.

The Moon shines bright
In time of night.

Nightingales sing
In time of spring.

The sturdy Oak, it was
the tree,
That saved his royal ma-
jesty.

Peter denies
His Lord, and cries.

Queen Esther comes in
royal state,
To save the Jews from
dismal fate.

Rachel doth mourn
For her first born.

Samuel anoints
Whom God appoints.

Time cuts down all,
Both great and small.

Uriah's lovely wife
Made David seek his life.

Whales in the sea
God's voice obey.

Xerxes the great did die,
And so must you and I.

Youth's forward slips
Death soonest nips.

Zaccheus did climb the
tree,
His Lord to see.

Can you see the Bible references just learning the ABC's? How about perhaps the most well-known bedtime prayer ever.

Now I lay me down to sleep,
I pray thee, Lord, my soul to keep.

If I should die before I wake,
I pray thee, Lord, my soul to take.

It is also interesting that many of the most prestigious universities in America were originally founded by ministers and religious leaders. Harvard and Yale were founded by the Puritans. Princeton was founded by the Presbyterians.[9] They were founded to train the future leaders including ministers. An early motto for Harvard was "Veritas Christo at Ecclesiae" translated "Truth for Christ and the Church".[10]

There was another interesting excerpt from the Rules and Precepts of Harvard in 1636. Rule 2 says:

2. Let every student be plainly instructed, and earnestly pressed to consider well the main end of his life and studies is, to know God and Jesus Christ which is eternal life, John 17:3, and therefore lay Christ in the bottom, as the only foundation of sound knowledge and learning. And seeing the Lord only giveth wisdom, let everyone seriously set himself by prayer in secret to seek it from Him Prov 2:3.[11]

Now, unfortunately, many of those institutions have traded God's wisdom for the wisdom of men.

The fear of the Lord is the beginning of wisdom, and knowledge of the Holy One is understanding. (Prov 9:10)

[9] Bodie Hodge, Harvard, Yale, Princeton, Oxford- Once Christian? Answers Magazine, (June 27, 2007).
[10] What is Harvard Motto? Need to Know, September 16, 2020.
[11] Dr. Stephen Flick, The Christian Founders of Harvard, Christian Heritage Fellowship, Sep 8, 2021.

Let no one deceive himself. If anyone among you seems to be wise in this age, let him become a fool that he may become wise. For the wisdom of this world is foolishness with God. For it is written, "He catches the wise in their own craftiness"; and again, "The Lord knows the thoughts of the wise, that they are futile." (I Cor 3:18-20)

But know this, that in the last days perilous times will come: For men will be lovers of themselves, lovers of money, boasters, proud, blasphemers, disobedient to parents, unthankful, unholy, unloving, unforgiving, slanderers, without self-control, brutal, despisers of good, traitors, headstrong, haughty, lovers of pleasure rather than lovers of God, having a form of godliness but denying its power. And from such people turn away! For of this sort are those who creep into households and make captives of gullible women loaded down with sins, led away by various lusts, always learning and never able to come to the knowledge of the truth. (2 Tim 3:1-7)

The Founding Fathers did not shun God and the Bible, they embraced it. That led to One Nation Under God and In God We Trust.

Quotes From our Founding Fathers

The case has been made here that our Founding Fathers believed in God and respected the Bible. Maybe the best evidence for this assertion is from what they actually said. The following are a few quotes from some of them.[12]

---

[12] Fairchild, Mary, "Quotes of the Founding Fathers on Religion", Learn Religions, Sep.7, 2021, Learningreligions.com/cChristian-quotes-of-the-founding-fathers-700789.

George Washington our first president:

"While we are zealously performing the duties of good citizens and soldiers, we certainly ought not to be inattentive to the higher duties of religion. To the distinguished character of Patriot, it should be our highest glory to add the more distinguished character of Christian." —The Writings of Washington, pp. 342-343.

John Adams 2nd U.S. President and Signer of the Declaration of Independence:

"Suppose a nation in some distant Region should take the Bible for their only law Book, and every member should regulate his conduct by the precepts there exhibited! Every member would be obliged in conscience, to temperance, frugality, and industry; to justice, kindness, and charity towards his fellow men; and to piety, love, and reverence toward Almighty God ... What a Eutopia, what a Paradise would this region be." — Diary and Autobiography of John Adams, Vol. III, p. 9.

Thomas Jefferson 3rd U.S. President, Drafter and Signer of the Declaration of Independence:

"God who gave us life gave us liberty. And can the liberties of a nation be thought secure when we have removed their only firm basis, a conviction in the minds of the people that these liberties are of the Gift of God? That they are not to be violated but with His wrath? Indeed, I tremble for my country when I reflect that God is just; that His justice cannot sleep forever..." —Notes on the State of Virginia, Query XVIII, p. 237.

"I am a real Christian – that is to say, a disciple of the doctrines of Jesus Christ." —The Writings of Thomas Jefferson, p. 385.

John Hancock 1st Signer of the Declaration of Independence:

"Resistance to tyranny becomes the Christian and social duty of each individual... Continue steadfast and, with a proper sense of your dependence on God, nobly defend those rights which heaven gave, and no man ought to take from us." —History of the United States of America, Vol. II, p. 229.

Benjamin Franklin Signer of the Declaration of Independence and Unites States Constitution:

"Here is my Creed. I believe in one God, the Creator of the Universe. That He governs it by His Providence. That He ought to be worshipped.

"That the most acceptable service we render to Him is in doing good to His other children. That the soul of man is immortal and will be treated with justice in another life respecting its conduct in this. These I take to be the fundamental points in all sound religion, and I regard them as you do in whatever sect I meet with them.

"As to Jesus of Nazareth, my opinion of whom you particularly desire, I think the system of morals and his religion, as he left them to us, is the best the world ever saw, or is likely to see.

"But I apprehend it has received various corrupting changes, and I have, with most of the present dissenters in England,

some doubts as to his divinity; though it is a question I do not dogmatize upon, having never studied it, and think it needless to busy myself with it now, when I expect soon an opportunity of knowing the truth with less trouble. I see no harm, however, in its being believed, if that belief has the good consequence, as probably it has, of making His doctrines more respected and more observed; especially as I do not perceive, that the Supreme takes it amiss, by distinguishing the unbelievers in his government of the world with any peculiar marks of his displeasure."
—Benjamin Franklin wrote this in a letter to Ezra Stiles, President of Yale University on March 9, 1790.

It should be noted here that from what he said of himself, he may not have been a Christian, but he did support and respect God and the Bible.

Samuel Adams Signer of the Declaration of Independence and Father of the American Revolution:

"And as it is our duty to extend our wishes to the happiness of the great family of man, I conceive that we cannot better express ourselves than by humbly supplicating the Supreme Ruler of the world that the rod of tyrants may be broken to pieces, and the oppressed made free again; that wars may cease in all the earth, and that the confusions that are and have been among nations may be overruled by promoting and speedily bringing on that holy and happy period when the kingdom of our Lord and Savior Jesus Christ may be everywhere established, and all people everywhere willingly bow to the scepter of Him who is Prince of Peace."

—*As Governor of Massachusetts, Proclamation of a Day of Fast, March 20, 1797.*

James Madison 4th U.S. President:

"*A watchful eye must be kept on ourselves lest while we are building ideal monuments of Renown and Bliss here, we neglect to have our names enrolled in the Annals of Heaven.*"
—*Written to William Bradford on November 9, 1772, Faith of Our Founding Fathers by Tim LaHaye, pp. 130-131; Christianity and the Constitution — The Faith of Our Founding Fathers by John Eidsmoe, p. 98.*

John Quincy Adams 6th U.S. President:

"*The hope of a Christian is inseparable from his faith. Whoever believes in the divine inspiration of the Holy Scriptures must hope that the religion of Jesus shall prevail throughout the earth. Never since the foundation of the world have the prospects of mankind been more encouraging to that hope than they appear to be at the present time. And may the associated distribution of the Bible proceed and prosper till the Lord shall have made 'bare His holy arm in the eyes of all the nations, and all the ends of the earth shall see the salvation of our God' (Isaiah 52:10).*"
—*Life of John Quincy Adams, p. 248.*

William Penn Founder of Pennsylvania:

"*I do declare to the whole world that we believe the Scriptures to contain a declaration of the mind and will of God in and to those ages in which they were written; being given forth by the Holy Ghost moving in the heart of holy men of*

God; that they ought also to be read, believed, and fulfilled in our day; being used for reproof and instruction, that the man of God may be perfect. They are a declaration and testimony of heavenly things themselves, and, as such, we carry a high respect for them. We accept them as the words of God Himself."
—Treatise of the Religion of the Quakers, p. 355.

Roger Sherman Signer of the Declaration of Independence and United States Constitution:

"I believe that there is one only living and true God, existing in three persons, the Father, the Son, and the Holy Ghost, the same in substance equal in power and glory. That the Scriptures of the Old and New Testaments are a revelation from God, and a complete rule to direct us how we may glorify and enjoy him. That God has foreordained whatsoever comes to pass, so as thereby he is not the author or approver of sin. That He creates all things and preserves and governs all creatures and all their actions, in a manner perfectly consistent with the freedom of will in moral agents, and the usefulness of means. That He made man at first perfectly holy, that the first man sinned, and as he was the public head of his posterity, they all became sinners in consequence of his first transgression, are wholly indisposed to that which is good and inclined to evil, and on account of sin are liable to all the miseries of this life, to death, and to the pains of hell forever.

"I believe that God having elected some of mankind to eternal life, did send His own Son to become man, die in the room and stead of sinners and thus to lay a foundation for the offer of pardon and salvation to all mankind, so as all may be saved who

are willing to accept the gospel offer: also by His special grace and spirit, to regenerate, sanctify and enable to persevere in holiness, all who shall be saved; and to procure in consequence of their repentance and faith in Himself their justification by virtue of His atonement as the only meritorious cause... —The Life of Roger Sherman, pp. 272-273.

Benjamin Rush Signer of the Declaration of Independence and Ratifier of the U.S. Constitution:

"The gospel of Jesus Christ prescribes the wisest rules for just conduct in every situation of life. Happy they who are enabled to obey them in all situations!" —The Autobiography of Benjamin Rush, pp. 165-166.

Alexander Hamilton Signer of the Declaration of Independence and Ratifier of the U.S. Constitution:

"I have carefully examined the evidence of the Christian religion, and if I was sitting as a juror upon its authenticity, I would unhesitatingly give my verdict in its favor." —Famous American Statesmen, p. 126.

Patrick Henry Ratifier of the U.S. Constitution:

"It cannot be emphasized too strongly or too often that this great nation was founded, not by religionists, but by Christians, not on religions, but on the gospel of Jesus Christ. For this very reason peoples of other faiths have been afforded asylum, prosperity, and freedom of worship here." —The Trumpet Voice of Freedom: Patrick Henry of Virginia, p. iii.

"The Bible... is a book worth more than all the other books that were ever printed." —Sketches of the Life and Character of Patrick Henry, p. 402.

John Jay 1st Chief Justice of the U.S. Supreme Court and President of the American Bible Society:

"By conveying the Bible to people thus circumstanced, we certainly do them a most interesting kindness. We thereby enable them to learn that man was originally created and placed in a state of happiness, but, becoming disobedient, was subjected to the degradation and evils which he and his posterity have since experienced.

"The Bible will also inform them that our gracious Creator has provided for us a Redeemer, in whom all the nations of the earth shall be blessed; that this Redeemer has made atonement 'for the sins of the whole world,' and thereby reconciling the Divine justice with the Divine mercy has opened a way for our redemption and salvation; and that these inestimable benefits are of the free gift and grace of God, not of our deserving, nor in our power to deserve." —In God We Trust—The Religious Beliefs and Ideas of the American Founding Fathers, p. 379."

CHAPTER 5
GOVERNMENT

Installation

The Founding Fathers knew what man was like. They knew they could not trust people to always do the "right thing" or make the right decisions. Any government that they set up had to have checks and balances to ensure that no one person or group could seize control. There had to be safeguards. Historically, they had seen the tyranny of self-centered power-hungry tyrants ruling. They knew how crowds could be stirred by story-telling charismatic leaders into unbelievable acts of violence. They knew the cruelty of people against other people even in the church; consider the historical witch hunts conducted by the church. They knew the church could not be trusted either. It was a daunting task.

The task was compounded by the fact that at that time there were thirteen individual colonies. Each had its own separate outlook and ways of doing things. Our former pastor referred to that thinking as the "DNA" of the organization. It would not be easy to combine the "DNA" of these separate colonies into one nation. They had to get the colonies to agree.

We call this nation **The United States of America**, but we have forgotten what that means. We are a combination of separate but equal states into one unified nation! We started with 13 colonies and the Founding Fathers somehow managed to unite those different colonies into one unified whole. It required the combination of separate colonial "DNAs" into a single national "DNA". The usual way to accomplish such a feat was that the stronger person or group conquered the weaker ones and forced submission. People who resisted were killed, imprisoned, or exiled. Our Founding Fathers did it while maintaining the separate DNA of each state! Now we are fifty United States of America! Their motto was *E Pluribus Unum*, out of many one. Were the Founding Fathers blessed in their efforts because they honored God?

When I was in high school, I took an advanced American history class. It was hard but incredibly inciteful. The textbook was Morrison and Commager's *The Growth of the American Republic* (yes, I remembered the textbook and author's names). The textbook was a two-volume set of thick books. There was also a good deal of outside reading. It was a lot of work, but history came alive. It was as though you were there watching the struggles, debates, and concerns at each major event in our history. These were real people. They were not just facts.

Our Founding Fathers were real people, with all the biases, opinions, and shortcomings exhibited in people today. They debated and got frustrated but they also prayed. The Founding Fathers pledged their lives and fortunes to the cause. They were determined. In one long sentence, they set the goals in the majestic **Preamble**:

> *We the people of the United States, in order to form a more perfect union, **establish justice**, **ensure domestic Tranquility**, **provide for the common defense**, **promote***

the general Welfare, and secure the Blessings of Liberty to ourselves and our Posterity, do ordain and establish this Constitution for the United States of America.

Balance

The Biblical view of men (and women) is that we are all sinners. They could see the shortcomings in each other, just as we can today. They needed to structure the government with a system of checks and balances so that no one individual or group could seize control. They decided to set up three separate entities: The Legislative, The Executive, and the Judicial Branches. Each was to have their assigned duties, and each was to be a check on the other two branches.

The **Legislative branch** was to make the laws. Even in this branch, the Founding Fathers wanted balance. The thirteen original states and those to be added later, all have their own "DNA". The Founding Fathers did not want states with large urban populations, for example, to overpower the more rural, less populated states. They wanted to preserve the union. Their solution was two separate legislative branches, one representing population (House of Representatives) and the second giving each state an equal voice (The Senate). Making new laws had to be hard. The legislature could not just ram a law through based on the emotions of the moment or who was in power. There had to be discussions and compromises to be successful. It would also be even harder to amend the Constitution once established. Think of how much worse it might have been to the Japanese citizens living in the United States after the attack on Pearl Harbor. If it were easy to change the laws, what would have happened to all the Muslims living in the US after 911. The Founding

Fathers wanted laws that made sense based on study and reflection and did not violate the other goals expressed in the Preamble.

Some in Congress now want to make the District of Columbia a separate state. Is this really wise? Is this what our Forefathers would have wanted? Consider that if Senators and Congressmen were elected from the same party from that new state. The other parties would not feel welcome in the very place they would have to work. The party in power could easily mobilize a crowd of emotional sheep to demonstrate against any disagreement with their viewpoint. They could also easily pass state laws to hinder any opposing demonstrations. Would that be fair? Wouldn't that create a super state above all the others? Such action is precisely the kind of thing a dictator would do to secure and maintain his power. Shouldn't the seat of the federal government be neutral ground? If it is not, could it become the very thing that destroys our precious democratic government?

The **Executive Branch** was to manage the country according to the established laws under the leadership of the President and Vice President. The Executive branch was not to make the laws. The President may, for example, send troops into a foreign country to quell an uprising, but could not declare war without the Legislative Branch's approval. The Founding Fathers wanted checks on the President so that they could not make themselves a "king" with unlimited power. The President could also exercise a veto on Congressional bills if the President felt it was warranted, another check. It is interesting that the Founding Fathers specified that the President and Vice President had to be citizens, at least thirty-five years old. Later Amendment 22 was added in 1951 limiting service to no more than two terms. They wanted presidents with maturity, some life experience, and a vested interest in the national welfare. They also did not want presidents to ever establish themselves as "kings". Might we learn a lesson from their wisdom and limit the terms in Congress as well and for the same reason? Politicians tend to establish mini "Kingdoms" of influence. Would we be better off with people in office who were more concerned with the welfare of the union than with their own wealth?

The **Judicial Branch** was to judge all cases under the Constitution. The Supreme Court was **NOT** authorized to change the Constitution. They were supposed to make sure that both the Legislative and Executive branches followed the guidelines of the Constitution. Many people today want to make changes to the Constitution. Their argument is that the old document is outdated, things have changed since it was written, and the Constitution needs to be changed accordingly. The Constitution dealt with broad topics on how we are to live and interact with each other. Has man really changed, though? He still kills. Early man did it with sticks and stones, now we can do it with highly sophisticated drone weapons operated by men thousands of miles away from the killing field. Man steals, just watch the news. He still commits adultery, lies, and is jealous, coveting what others have. He is still self-centered. None of these things have changed. The legislature certainly can make new laws based on the principles of the Constitution to cover man's new inventions. The car, the internet, the airplane, etc. were not known by the Founding Fathers. The legislature has the right and should pass laws governing those things. The Constitution is the foundation. Shouldn't the foundation be difficult to change? Unfortunately, some people find the normal route unacceptable and try to force change through the Supreme Court. The Supreme Court was never meant to be the Legislative branch. Is their job to change the Constitution or uphold it and protect the vision of the Founding Fathers? There is a process in place to amend the Constitution. It should be hard so that the majority of people get behind the change. It should never be forced on everyone by a few. Perhaps one amendment we might consider is the impeachment of Supreme Court justices that step outside their responsibilities under the Constitution.

The Founding Fathers also sought balance between the powers of the Federal Government and individual and state rights. The Bill of Rights was ratified in 1791. The **First Amendment** protected religion, free speech, and the right to assemble. There are those who want to eradicate references to God in public. They want to eliminate news stations that are God oriented and present an opposing viewpoint to the Godless atheistic religion. Such efforts are contrary to the first amendment. Every news station is biased because they are made up of people who are biased. Everyone has a world view. It is part of who you are. Freedom of speech is an extremely important right and must be protected. We do not have to agree with everything or everybody, but the only way to achieve balance is to allow all viewpoints to be expressed.

We must be careful which "experts" we listen to. All news media tell stories. They all choose which stories and statistics they want to emphasize. That is why we need all media viewpoints so that we can get a better picture of what is true and what is not. Should we also judge based on personalities? One politician may have a more likable demeaner, but that does not mean that person is a better candidate or would do a better job. We need to look closely at the track record. We also need to evaluate what they say about issues, not what they say about each other. "Mudslinging" does not clarify it clouds things.

Mark Twain wrote a story once called "Running For Governor". In it, his name was placed on the ballot for a governorship. After that, there were all kinds of stories in the newspapers about the terrible things he had done in the past. None of it was true. There was story after story. In the end, he decided to withdraw his nomination because he could not vote for such a terrible person! It seems like things have not changed much since then.

The **Second Amendment** protects the right to bear arms. In other nations, it appears that the first step in forcing citizens to submit to a small group bent on taking over the country is to take away each citizens ability to defend themselves. I have never owned a gun. The way the country is going, though, I may decide to buy one.

Let me say one other thing about guns. It is not guns that kill people. People kill people. If I owned a gun, I would still sleep quite well at night with the gun in the house. I know that gun would never load a magazine, place a shell in the chamber, point itself at me, and pull the trigger. I would only worry if there was an unstable person in the house with access to the gun. Restricting the ability to buy guns only limits the number of guns in the hands of responsible people. Does it really limit the number of guns in the hands of those who seek to do harm? We need better ways to identify those people. Those who seek to do harm can always find a gun.

Government by Reason NOT Emotion

The Founders knew what mobs could do. When emotion flairs, almost any atrocity is possible. People murder, steal, maim, shout obscenities and can be extremely cruel to others. When things calm down, many will regret what they did and said, but then it may be too late. The damage is done and may not be repairable. The Founding Fathers knew this. They saw it in themselves as they debated the issues. They wanted a government that was of the people, for the people, and by consent of the people, but they knew it would not happen based on the emotion of the people. Decisions had to be based on reason NOT emotion. They had to make it difficult to pass legislation or make changes so that the emotional flare-ups would not drive the process. Reason and compromise had to be the rule.

Amendment Ten limits the powers of the Federal Government to only those delegated to it by the Constitution. Others not prohibited by the Constitution are reserved for the States. Again, the Founding Fathers were seeking balance between federal and state's rights. Sometimes the President and Congress needs to be reminded that we are the **United States of America**. We have 50 separate "DNAs" combined into one fragile union. We went through a horrible costly Civil War in our history at one point when individual states felt their rights were being trampled on and they seceded from the union. We still bear the scars. Unfortunately, some shortsighted people want to eliminate those reminders. Is that wise? Others much smarter than me have stated that to ignore history or try to cover it up only leads to repeating that history. Rewriting history is not good either. Shouldn't the monuments be used instead to help teach the next generation about our history, both the good and the bad? The

Biblical viewpoint is that we are all sinners and make mistakes, but we are also just one race, the human race. We need to forgive each other for past mistakes and move on with our brothers and sisters.

There was one amendment that failed and illustrates why it should be hard to amend the Constitution. That was the **18th Amendment** outlawing alcohol in the United States. It was pushed through by religious groups who felt drunkenness was causing many of our problems. It was an extreme measure. Mark Twain said:

> *Prohibition only drives drunkenness behind doors and into dark places and does not cure it or even diminish it. (1867)*[13]

Was he right? A case can be made that those who pushed for outlawing alcohol were misinterpreting the Bible. Jesus, after all, turned water into wine at the wedding of Cana in Galilee and it was considered the best wine of all (John 2:1-11). Criminals like Al Capone capitalized on the 14th amendment to build their empires. Can you legislate morality? Fourteen years later the amendment was repealed.

They wanted balance even in the election of the president. They set up an electoral college to accomplish that end. Every presidential election we are reminded again that we are **The United States of America** NOT a dictatorship under the president. Each state needs to feel that they are represented and that their votes count. If the president is elected by strictly popular vote, then those states with larger populations would dominate every presidential election. The more rural less populist states might have virtually no say in who gets to be president. Less you think I am exaggerating here, I went

---

[13] Mark Twain, quoted by Turning Point USA, The Constitution of the United States of America, p. 52

online and looked up the populations in all 50 states. The chart that follows summarizes the results.

15 largest states	180.91 million	61.96 %
15 next largest states	77.27 million	26.47 %
20 lowest population states	33.79 million	11.57 %
Total	291.97 million	

Of course, the numbers are the total population, but they also reflect the relative sizes of the voting population. Let's suppose that 51 % of the voting population in the 15 largest states voted for candidate A. That would be 31.6 % (61.96 % X .51) of the total national voting population. The total voting population in the 35 lowest population states is only 38.04 % (26.47 + 11.47 %). In order for the 35 lower population states to elect a different candidate into office, over 83 % (31.6 /38.04 X 100) of the voting population would have to vote for the alternative candidate. That is virtually an impossibility! The 35 lowest population states would always be at the mercy of the most populist states. In fact, the politicians would probably only campaign in the 15 largest states. The electoral college was designed to prevent this and allow all states to participate. I heard a Hillsdale college professor say that the president was to be elected by the "most votes in the most states". It also allowed that the president may not receive the most popular votes. He or she, however, would be the best candidate for the most states. The control would be in the hands of all the people in all the states.

The Constitution is paradoxical most of all about power, which it grants and withholds, bestows and limits, aggregates and divides, liberates and restrains. Elections are staggered, so as to distribute them across time. The founding document also divides power across space; the people grant a share of their natural authority to the federal government, but another share to the states where they live.[14]

Participation

The **26th Amendment** guaranteed all citizens the right to vote at 18 years of age. That is a precious right. It was ratified in 1971. At that time, 18-year-old men faced the draft as we were at war with North Vietnam. The idea was that if you were old enough to be drafted you were old enough to vote. I was 25. I had a steady job since I was 16. That was true of most of the people I knew. The typical family was one in which one parent, usually the father, worked while the other stayed home with the children. Usually there was only one car in the family. It was rare that the family income could support private schools or college education. If you wanted to go, you had to begin preparing as a freshman in high school, get good grades, and score well on SAT tests to get accepted into college. In New York, where I grew up, you could get a scholarship to a state school if you scored high enough on the SAT test. Even with a scholarship, you still had to work and take out student loans to cover the cost. 18-year old's during that time were forced into maturing earlier than today. Today parents tend to subsidize their children sometimes well into the twenties. Does it scare you that the right to vote has been given to those who have yet to become productive members of society?

[14] Larry P. Arnn, "The Electoral College Is Anything But Outdated", The Wall Street Journal, Nov 14, 2016.

The right to vote must be encouraged and protected. Part of that protection means that we make every effort to ensure that only those with the legal right to vote can vote. Should anyone be allowed to vote who is not a citizen? Should we allow someone to vote as someone else? Is it right to allow people to use false documents to cast a vote? Shouldn't every citizen present proper identification to prove they have the right to vote? What efforts are being made to ensure that no one votes more than once? If any of these things are violated, how can we trust the results? No one should be forced to vote one way or another but shouldn't the scrutiny of the right to vote be flawless?

Ballots Not Bullets

Our whole system of government is based on voting. Our Founding Fathers wanted the people to make big decisions as to who would be elected, laws enacted, and amendments ratified. It was to be ballots not bullets. Everyone was to abide by the result of the vote. People can only abide by the vote if they feel the vote was honest. If discrepancies are not fully investigated, how then can the vote be trusted? Shouldn't such incidents be fully investigated and prosecuted even if it would not affect the final outcome? All sides must be united in this. Do we want bullets instead of ballots?

Taxation

The government gets its revenue primarily through taxes. It should be proportionate; that way the rich do pay more actual dollars and the poor less. Here is a thought, should every citizen have to pay some tax? Why should anyone be given the right to influence or say how the taxes are spent if they have not contributed to the pot? That would be like giving kids the right to tell their parents how to spend the money the parents earn. If you are going to be a citizen, then take on the responsibilities of a citizen. The tax does not have to be exorbitant, just something.

Are the tax laws too cumbersome and should they be simplified? Our previous President made some headway on that front early in his tenure. Now it is easier for many without having to save all those receipts for every gift deduction; the basic deduction is sufficient. It is easier for many and much simpler for the IRS. It seems today that the IRS could use all the help it can get. A simplified tax program would be something where everyone paid a certain percentage of their income after all deductions. If there is no income, then the citizen pays the minimum amount.

Just out of curiosity, I looked up the latest stats off the internet (year 2018) about our Federal Income Tax data.

Who paid the taxes? The following chart summarize the results:[15]

FIGURE 1.
Half of Taxpayers Pay 97 Percent of Federal Income Taxes
Share of Adjusted Gross Income and federal income taxes paid by income group in 2018

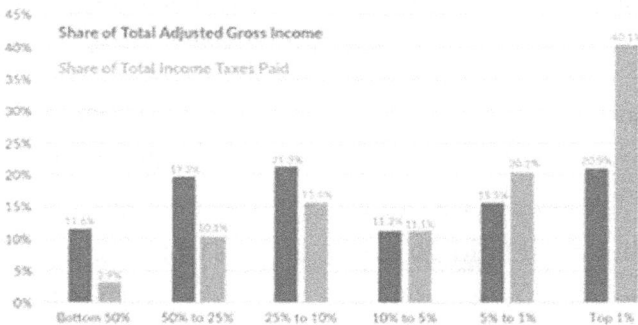

Source: IRS, Statistics of Income, Individual Income Rates and Tax Shares.

---

[15] Taken and condensed from Erica York, Summary of the Latest Income Tax Data 2021 Update, February 2021.

According to the chart, the top 50 % of the taxpayers in 2018 earned 88.4 % of the total income but paid 97.1% of the total taxes. The bottom 50% earned 11.6% of the total but only paid 2.9% of the taxes. Also, the top 1% paid a higher percentage of the taxes (40.1%) than the total taxes paid by the bottom 90% (28.6%)[16]. How then can we justify making the rich pay more taxes? Maybe a better case can be made that the bottom 50% are not paying their fair share. Why then are we always going after the rich to pay more taxes?

There was another interesting fact that only a small amount of the total taxes are collected through the corporate income tax. A friend of mine who owned his company explained why. An owner of a corporation pays taxes first on the gross earnings of his corporation. Let us say for the moment, that was 21 %. Now 79% of his earnings are passed on to him. If he had a really good year, then his individual tax rate may be 37% (2017). That means that he paid:

21% + 37% X 79% = Total 50%

Why should any hard-working owner of a company have to give half of his income to the government? Probably the majority of such companies may be relatively small business owners.

Is it surprising that many of these people seek as many ways as possible to shelter their income? First, they may pay bonuses to people in the company to reduce the corporate tax. The largest portion will and should go to the owners of the company. The rest goes to the employees. Owners are quite willing to give say 10 percent of the profits to the employees. If the corporate tax is 21%, they save 11 % on bonus dollars. They are happy and the employees

---

16 Top 10 % paid 71.4% so the bottom 90% paid 100%-71.4% = 28.6%

are happy. After that, they will look for ways to shelter their personal earnings. Sheltering still costs money but if you can pay someone 25% to shelter money to avoid paying 37%, the owner pockets an additional 12% of the sheltered income. The IRS, by the way, loses taxes on that sheltered income. If the IRS lowered the tax rate to say 22% and it would cost the businessman the same 25% to shelter the income, likely he would just pay the taxes. He gains 3%. The IRS increases their income. That is what our previous President tried to do. Raising taxes on the wealthy may not solve anything.

Management

I think a better solution is the same as for individual households, manage better what you have coming in. We as individuals cannot live beyond our means. How then can the Federal Government do so? Now I know there can be lean times and the government may have to borrow to get through it. Shouldn't that be the exception not the norm? When things are better, pay back the loans. That is what any financial planner will tell you to do. The Bible tells us the borrower is servant to the lender (Proverbs 22:7). Every loan that is paid off means that the interest paid on that loan is now available to fund other things.

Here is a thought, how about attaching a cost factor to every new bill introduced in Congress. As individuals we may want to buy a new Ferrari but when we look at our income, we may only be able to afford a Ford or nothing at all. Local governments put items on the ballot for taxpayers to pay for improvements with a tax increase. The voters then make the decision. Perhaps the Federal Government should do the same.

How about streamlining or even eliminating departments. The IRS is a classic case. The IRS workload appears to be overwhelming at present. Perhaps the IRS could use an overhaul. The end result could make the department more efficient and save the government money.

The same thing can be done with other departments. Maybe some departments are obsolete or can be combined. When businesses are taking in less than their expenses, they look for ways to cut expenses, do more with less, or generate additional income. They never just leave everything as status quo. If they do, they will go out of business.

Here is another thought, maybe those in the government could curtail some spending on perks and benefits or even donate some money. It may not make a big dent in the shortfall but would set an example to every government employee and the public that getting spending under control is a priority. Remember the Founding Fathers. They pledged their fortunes to the cause, and some lost them in the process. Are our elected representatives really there to make our nation better or are they just there for what they can get? I heard President John F. Kennedy say:

> *"Ask not what the country can do for you but what you can do for the country."*

Differences

Our Founding Fathers quickly realized that individual rights must be protected. They added to the Constitution a Bill of Rights to protect the individual. They added freedom of religion, freedom of speech, freedom of the press, freedom of assembly (Amendment One). They protected the right to bear arms (Amendment Two). They protected individuals against unreasonable searches and seizures (Amendment Four). They set down the rules for due process of law (Amendment Five). If someone was indicted, they protected the right to a speedy trial (Amendment Six). They provided for the right to a trial by jury in civil lawsuits (Amendment Seven). Individuals were protected against excessive fines, excessive bail, and cruel and unusual punishment (Amendment Eight). Individuals were to be protected against the heavy hand of those in power. They had witnessed that heavy hand as they struggled to survive as colonies. If this new United States of America were to survive, the individual had to be protected.

Are those freedoms being eroded by those in powerful positions? I have freedom of speech. Does that mean I can only express agreement with those in power or do I have the right to disagree? Do I have the right to assemble with others who disagree? It is also inherent in the freedom that I should not face reprisals against me for disagreeing. Sadly, though, many are being ostracized, often severely if they voice disagreement with those in power. I am not speaking just of those in powerful government positions, but also those who hold power because of their wealth and status in private institutions and companies.

This is not justification for angry outbursts of vehement, hurtful, word inciting speech against those we disagree with. Can anyone justify mob violence against others? We all have world views (chapter 2) often different from each other. That is part of who we are. We all should respect those views even if they disagree with our own. Respect, though, does not mean we must always agree. In today's world, though, if you disagree, it is often viewed as "hate" speech. If you disagree on some issues, it may lead to belittling attacks, slights to your intelligence, or in more extreme cases, loud angry outbursts to drown out what you have to say. If we cannot disagree civilly with each other, then how can we ever work together or come to a compromise where compromises are possible?

Let me use two current controversial examples to make my points.

The first one is the abortion issue. Let's be honest here and not hide the real issue with misleading rhetoric. Both sides are making a choice. One side says a woman should have the right to terminate the life of the fetus. The opposing view is that she should not have that right. There is a lot of hype about rape and incest. According to a recent USA Today article, rape, or incest only account for only 1.5 % of all abortions[17]. That means that 98.5 % percent are just for convenience. Even if we allow abortions for rape and incest, why should the fetus have to give up their life as a solution to her unwanted pregnancy problem? There are intelligent passionate people on both sides of the issue. This issue is also a clash of world views. If the subject of abortion comes up, shouldn't we still express our views with civility and respect? I found, though, that if a person does not have a good logical, scientific basis for their viewpoint, they belittle and shout down those with the opposing view.

The second controversial topic is the alternate lifestyles expressed by the LBTGQ movement. This also is a conflict of world views. If you believe there is no God or God only has minimal involvement in the world, then we have all just evolved to where we are now. It

---

[17] Alia E. Dastagir, "Rape and Incest Account for Hardly Any Abortions. So Why Are They Now a Focus?", USA Today, May 24, 2019.

follows that any different lifestyles are just part of that process, and all lifestyles are just personal preferences. If, on the other hand, God is the Creator and He is very involved in this world, then He is in charge, and we should all abide by His rules. Both views of origins as I have stated earlier in chapter 2, are belief systems. Our Founding Fathers believed in God and the Bible as His "owner's manual" describing His rules for His creation. The obvious ones we are all familiar with are the Ten Commandments. The homosexual lifestyle is not new to the Bible either. There are references all the way back in the books of Moses among the first books written (Examples: Gen 19:1-4; Lev 18:22, 20:13). It is also in the New Testament (Rom 1:18-26; I Cor 6:9-10). Those references are generally not favorable to the practice. Please do not take my word for it. Check it out for yourself. Belief systems are protected under the First Amendment. No one has the right to dictate our beliefs. I do not have the right to force you to believe in God and the Bible. Those that believe in LGBTQ lifestyles do not have the right to force that belief on those of us who disagree. I think it also applies to Gay Pride celebrations. Should I be forced to agree, support, and even participate in such celebrations? Some companies feel they have that right and bring consequences on employees that resist.

We should be civil to each other and respect each other but we do not have to agree with each other. At a party one time I was introduced to a man with an alternate lifestyle. According to those who worked with him, he had a great work ethic. I complemented him on it. I was civil to him and did not try to "preach" to him about his lifestyle. That is his choice. I needed to respect him even if I did not agree with him. It is not for me to judge another (Matt 7:1). God is the judge (Heb 9:27).

Both of the previous examples can have political consequences. It is the right of those in opposition to present their viewpoints. Then the voters decide. That is our system. Is it right, though, for either side to try to coerce, intimidate, or belittle the voter or negate their properly presented vote? That vote is precious! Shouldn't that vote be protected? Ballots or bullets!

Justice

Our Founding Fathers protected the rights of the individual, but they also balanced that with a system of government to make laws that were to be obeyed by the individuals. It is a constant balancing act to make sure individual rights are not compromised and at the same time convict and punish those that are guilty of a crime. Lady Justice is often presented as having a balance in one hand and a sword in the other.

An individual accused of a crime was to be brought before the court system and that system was to discern guilt or innocence (the scale) and if necessary, apply punishment (the sword). The prosecuting and defense attorneys are to present their cases with the ultimate goal of discerning the truth. The juries are to listen to both sides and then render a verdict on guilt or innocence or proper punishment. It isn't a perfect system, but it is the best we have. It may be the best system of justice in the world. Isn't it a whole lot better than dictatorial justice or mob rule? It is run, though, by imperfect people. Criminals try to thwart justice by hiding evidence, intimidation, or just plain lies. Sometimes in their frustration, the police do not do things exactly right and evidence is tainted or lost. Some are convicted that should not be while others should be and are not. For the most part, though, it works.

The system was meant to be fair and unbiased. Unfortunately, it seems that more and more people are being prosecuted for political reasons and not for legitimate crimes. Politicians seem to be going out of their way to seek "dirt" on an opponent that could lead to some kind of prosecution. They then go out of their way to make sure that all the lawyers, the judges, the media etc. are completely in agreement. Woe to anyone that should have a different opinion. Woe to anybody that really wants to know all the facts before making any judgement. Sometimes the facts do not even seem to be relevant. The irony of it all is that many of those bringing the charges appear to be guilty of the same things! I am reminded of the story in John 8:1-11, where a woman is caught in adultery and the Jewish leaders bring her before Jesus in an attempt to trick Him. I always thought it took two to commit adultery, but the man is never brought before Him. Jesus does not respond immediately, but when He does, He says:

> ”He who is without sin among you, let him throw a stone at her first.” (John 8:7)

One by one beginning with the oldest, all the men left. She was left alone with Jesus and He did not condemn her. One simple phrase and Jesus was able to reveal their hypocrisy. Maybe we should put a rock on all the podiums in our government. Would they get the hint? Somehow, I doubt it. When the storytellers have succeeded in stirring up the emotions, reason and common sense vanish.

As of this writing, there is a lot of hype in the news against a political leader concerning his conduct while in office. The phrase "nobody is above the law" is constantly being touted. I would tend to agree, but I would strongly caution those who vehemently oppose him to be very careful in indicting him. A conviction in such a case is also a court precedent. That means that anyone else guilty of the same conduct can also be tried as well. If many of the other political leaders have or will do the same thing, shouldn't they also be tried as well? After all, shouldn't the phrase "nobody is above the law" apply to everyone not just your political rivals?

Once a fair and unbiased trial has been completed and a guilty verdict is rendered, the government has the right to punish the wrongdoer. Here is question though, should the system invoke the most extreme penalties, death, for the most extreme premeditated murder crimes? There may be mitigating "circumstances" if someone were to kill someone in a rage or on something that influence their behavior in the moment. How can there be any "mitigating circumstances when it is thought out before hand, carefully planned, and executed? Ignorance of the law is no excuse either. Giving such people life instead of the death penalty, means they will be heroes in the eyes of others who are thinking of doing the same thing. Meanwhile, we the people have to pay for their support for the rest of their lives.

CHAPTER 6
IMMIGRANTS

Assimilate

Consider why people emigrate to the United States. Most come to better their lives, escape persecution, to be able worship as they choose, etc. If their country of origin was so good, why would they want to emigrate? If they come here, why should our nation accept the traditions and wisdom that may well have contributed to the conditions that made them decide to leave their homeland? They need to assimilate and accept the foundational principles that made the United States great. I have traced my ancestry. My distant relatives came from the United Kingdom and Central Europe. I suspect that if you do the same, most of you will find the same thing. Remember the famous quote on the Statue of Liberty by Emma Lazarus:

> "Give me your tired, your poor, your huddled masses yearning to breathe free, The wretched refuse of your teeming shore. Send these, the homeless, tempest-tossed to me, I lift my lamp beside the golden door!"

Should we welcome them? Should every effort be made to assimilate them wherever possible? Do they have the right to our land, our things, our medical facilities, our medicines, or anything else in America? They are guests. We should treat them with respect and dignity. They can ask to enter our country, but they cannot demand that we take them in. It all must be done lawfully.

Americans have always been generous and try to help people in need. When disaster strikes almost anywhere in the world Americans send aid. Bible believing Christians are among the first to do so. Right now, though, people are storming our borders trying to illegally enter. I understand the need but is storming the gates the answer?

Makeover Not Takeover

There is a process whereby an immigrant can enter the United States legally and even become a citizen if they desire. Perhaps the government should look into streamlining that process. Should we really grant amnesty to everyone that storms our gates when others have obeyed our laws and entered legally? I know there are hardships for some, and persecution. The sheer numbers are causing problems and resentment from citizens. Many immigrants are being given things free that are not available to many citizens in this country. Is that right?

Every country has a right to secure their borders. We have even given money to other countries to do so. Shouldn't we have the right to do the same thing to control the entry into our land? We have far too many people trying to take advantage of us.

While people from another country bring with them another language, customs, different foods, etc., that is normal. Is it right, though, that those immigrants demand that we citizens do everything the way they have done it? They are to assimilate with us not the other way around. If we were to move to Germany, we would expect to have to learn the German language. We would not expect Germans to learn English. We might appreciate those Germans who spoke to us in English, but eventually we would have to learn some German. We would also expect to have to obey their laws and customs; we would not expect them to follow our rules. Initially we may seek to live with those that are like us, but eventually we need to assimilate into the German culture.

Every immigrant community started out clustering in specific areas within cities. Those neighborhoods also became a source of problems for the cities. Gangs arose. There was often violence between rival immigrant groups. Drugs and other illegal activities often sprang up in those groups. An individual could avoid the problems by leaving the group and fully assimilating into the general society. There is another way. Clean up the neighborhood and make it an attraction, a desirable place to visit. In that case, the immigrant neighborhood is assimilating by inviting the rest of the nation in. It only works, though, if the rest of the citizens feel safe, respected, and welcome.

There is evidence of all kinds of ethnic groups around me. When I walk around, I hear all different languages. We all get along. I feel safe. I feel comfortable striking up a conversation with anyone of them. There are, unfortunately, certain areas in the city that are not safe. Those areas seem to be the center of much of the crime in the city. That is sad. At one time, there were a lot of those ethnic neighborhoods, and each was looked down upon until they were assimilated. Now we recognize the heritage, but a lot of the prejudice arising from the new group entering the US is gone. Each group in our country's history had to prove that they would be valuable additions to the nation. Each had to show a good work ethic, that they respected the existing laws, and respected the rest of our nation's citizens. Over time most of the groups overcame any initial resistance to entering the country. Some groups of our brothers and sisters just have not completely assimilated. Respect is earned by giving respect. The Bible calls it reaping what you sow. Is prejudice innate or is it learned by how others treat us?

Earn Not Deserve

Do illegal immigrants automatically have the right to our jobs, our medicine, or any other privilege we all share as citizens? Do they have the right to demand those things? Legal immigrants are guests, and we share our privileges. Most Americans are sympathetic to the plight of those who are persecuted or suffering hardship, but that does not mean that everyone undergoing such things should automatically be allowed into our country.

Rather than just wholesale granting amnesty or the right to citizenship, perhaps we institute a system of sponsorship whereby citizens in good standing can sponsor an immigrant. Under such a system, the citizen accepts responsibility for the immigrant. They would help in all aspects of the immigrant's entry into this country, where they will stay, how they will support themselves, and so forth. They would also need to accept responsibility for their actions and the consequences of those actions. Potential immigrants could ask for such sponsorship ahead of time. Sponsorship could expedite the process. The goal is better control. We are flooded with immigrants and the need is to funnel them into the legal process and prevent unwanted people from entering. Are sanctuary cities the right solution? Do they solve the problem or just create more ghettos with more crime?

Do immigrants have the right to demand citizenship? Citizenship is a privilege and must be earned. It takes time. It takes work. It takes study to learn our history, our heritage, and our laws. There is a process, and any legal immigrant can apply to become a citizen. Do it right and they assimilate. They become valued partners in this great American Nation. Do it wrong and they just become pawns in a political process.

CHAPTER 7
FACTS OF LIFE

The title of this chapter sounds like we are about to talk to an adolescent about the "birds and the bees". Actually, it has nothing to do with that discussion. There are just some things that are true about living and existing in this world.

Preparation

We need to prepare for events in life so that we can avoid being a burden to our families or the country. That same Bible also contains wisdom for daily living.

Life

Every person needs to prepare for life. When you are young, parents' guide, protect and provide. Eventually, though, everyone must take their place in society. They must earn a living and support themselves. No one gets a free ride.

Death

The fact is we are all going to die. There are no survivors to the experience of life. If you believe in God and the Bible, then you know there will be a future time of death and judgement. If the atheist is correct and death is the end, Bible believers will never know they were wrong. If, on the other hand, the Bible is correct and judgement is coming, all of us will know it. Is waiting and taking your chances really a good idea?

Shouldn't we prepare for death? There are ads on TV all the time about a "Ten Dollar" plan to buy life insurance to handle those final expenses. The implication is that it will only cost you ten dollars a month and all the expenses are covered. That is nonsense. Insurance companies are in the business to make money. They know the life expectancy of individuals at every age. They have to charge a premium that brings in more money for any age group than what they expect to pay out for deaths. Assume for the moment that final expenses are about $10,000. In addition, let's suppose, for example, a person is 75 years old and based on the statistics, he might expect to live on average another 15 years. If the insurance company charges $10 per month ($120 per year) the insurance company will take in $1800 over 15 years. That is nowhere near the $10,000 expected final expense. If the company is to make any money over the fifteen years, they can only grant maybe $1,000 life insurance for the $10 per month premium. To cover the full final expense, the insured would have to pay about $100 per month. Ads tell stories and the people telling them make money doing it. The storytellers may not be experts, and they may not be giving you the whole picture. Isn't it better to prepare for final expenses ahead of time? My dad and stepmom living only on social security managed to pay their funeral costs ahead of time in monthly installments. There were no out-of-pocket expenses when they passed.

What about the legacy we leave to our families. Did we say everything we needed to say? Did we forgive, encourage, give directions, etc. Do those left behind know how we feel, how much we love them, and how we think of them? The patriarchs of the Bible passed on their thoughts and wishes.

Aging

In between life and death is another fact of life; we are going to get older. When we do, we often find that we cannot do the same things we used to do when we were younger. Wow, what a shock! We need to prepare for the later years when we cannot do things or compete at the same level as a younger person. Sports athletes know this all too well. Many are over the hill before they reach their 40's. It also happens in more common jobs as well. The roofer finds it is not so easy to continue climbing ladders to repair and replace roofs. The electrician begins to feel the pains of aging as they pull wires through conduits as they grow older. It happens with those that work inside in air conditioning as well. We get tired. We may find we "run out of gas" easier as we age. The Bible clearly indicates that man should work. Many want to work. It is part of their identity. The work, though, may change as we get older. We need to prepare for that.

Part of that preparation should be to take away the stress associated with having to work. Pay off the debts so that we are no longer slaves to them. Save money as well, short term to help pay for things that wear out and long term toward retirement. It is sad to hear of athletes earning incredible amounts of money during their productive years and have little left in the later years. They may earn in one or two years what the rest of us take a lifetime to earn.

The Bible plan appears to involve some inheritance from parents to children, but it also came with a stipulation. The eldest son was supposed to get a double portion of the inheritance. The extra amount was supposed to be used to take care of the parents in their senior years. It was part of the commandment to honor your father and your mother. Now families are in turmoil. If there is an inheritance, there may be a lot of fighting over it. Children may not want to or cannot take care of their parents in the declining years. Many people are not preparing for those senior years.

Preparation is possible. Over time anyone can become a millionaire and not by winning the lottery. It takes discipline to save a specified amount regularly over time in a good established financial institution. Banks are probably not the best for long-term savings; mutual fund companies are better with better rates of return over time. The chart that follows illustrates what saving $100 or $200 per month would produce over time at various rates of return.

	45 years	
Return	$100/mo.	200/mo.
2% / year	$87,466	$174,931
6% / year	$275,599	$551,198
7% / year	$379,259	$758,519
8% /year	$527,454	**$1,054,908**

The first row illustrates why banks are not the best savings institutions over the long haul; they may not even pay 2%. Young people today with no experience can easily earn $10-$15 dollars an hour. That translates into $400-$600 per week or over $1600-$2400 per month. The Bible continually refers to a tithe or 10% as a standard for giving back to God. Many young people today could afford the $100 or even $200 per month applied to a savings plan. They just need to discipline themselves. If the 16-year-old started saving at age 16 and saved just \$100/month at an 8% rate of return, it would grow to over \$793,000 by the time they reach retirement age in 50 years. It would grow to over \$1.58 million at \$200/month. One of my grandsons worked while he was in college and managed to save \$8000. It can be done.

The longer you wait to save, the more money must be set aside each month to reach the million-dollar goal. Better rates of return also help. The next chart illustrates.

Goal \$1,000,000		
Rate of Return	#Years	Amt/mo
4% per year	10	\$6791
	20	\$2726
	30	\$1441
6% per year	10	\$6102
	20	\$2164
	30	\$995
8% per year	10	\$5466
	20	\$1698
	30	\$671

If you get nothing else from the chart, realize it is important to start now. Waiting just makes things harder. Most good companies now offer 401K plans that allow you to automatically deduct a percentage of your income and put it in the plan. Some companies even match a portion of what you put in. If you do not take advantage of that, you are leaving money on the table. This is doable but it requires discipline. It requires you to live within your means. My wife and I are retired and now living on income derived from a 401K plan.

Social Security is another concern. That government plan was never a savings plan. Workers pay into it to provide benefits for those now retired. Children are paying for the benefits to their parents. When the plan was initiated, there were at least 30 maybe more people paying into the plan for everyone receiving benefits. Today it is about 3 for every one receiving benefits. When the plan started, it was expected that senior citizens would only live maybe 3-5 years beyond retirement. Now people are living much longer. There are real concerns that Social Security may not be sustainable over the long term. The younger generation are the ones most affected. Shouldn't they especially plan for their senior years?

Once you have achieved your goal and paid off your debt, the savings can now be translated into retirement income. The government requires that a portion of the 401K plan be taken as income once someone reaches a certain age. If the plan is in a good savings company, the value of the account can still increase even with the distribution. You can still work if you wish and many do. You are in control. There is a certain pride and satisfaction in being more independent. My wife and I like not being a burden to our children. We like the fact that we can share some of what we have with our children and others.

Life Insurance

Life insurance is an oxymoron. No one can ensure a longer life; it is really death insurance. You pay a premium so that you can recover the loss of income provided by the one that is insured. That is the major reason for such insurance. When you are young, usually you do not have a lot of savings. You may be living paycheck to paycheck. You may have a lot of debt. You may have just started your family. If the breadwinner dies, it is a disaster for that family. Life insurance provides a way to take care of that family in case of premature death. It does cost more for certain lifestyle choices like smoking, excessive weight, or engaging in dangerous activities, but it is still affordable when people are young. It makes good sense to have it on the breadwinners while the family is building toward financial independence. Does it make sense, though, to put any more than a burial amount on a child that is not contributing to the family financially?

Vocation

The Bible viewpoint is that God is the owner of all things and though we may work for others, He ultimately is our employer.

Therefore, whether you eat or drink, or whatever you do, do all to the glory of God. (I Corinthians 10:31)

The principle still applies even if we are the owners of a company because ultimately everything belongs to God.

Masters, give your bondservants what is just and fair, knowing that you also have a Master in heaven. (Colossians 4:1)

A bondservant was hired help and so this reference is to the relationship between the employers (masters) and employees (bondservants). There is an equally strong admonition to the bondservants.

Bondservants, be obedient to those who are your masters according to the flesh, with fear and trembling, in sincerity of heart, as to Christ; not with eyeservice, as men pleasers, but as bondservants of Christ, doing the will of God from the heart, with goodwill doing service, as to the Lord, and not to men, knowing that whatever good anyone does, he will receive the same from the Lord, whether he is a slave or free. (Ephesians 6:5-8)

God is the real boss. He wants both employers and employees to treat each other with respect following the same commandments that He gave to Moses. We should not lie. We should not steal. Taking something from a company that does not belong to us is stealing. Coming in late, leaving early, taking excessive breaks are all forms of stealing. If an employer does not pay the wages due to the employee, he is stealing. If God exists, He sees it all.

Those seeking employment should also recognize that jobs never come from the poor. They come from the rich. The rich man has the excess money that he can use to hire those less fortunate than himself. Anything that you do to reduce the wealth of the rich man also reduces his ability to provide jobs. If you try to make him pay more taxes for example, he may have to reduce his labor force or increase the prices of his products to make up for the loss. Either way those seeking employment are the ones affected as well.

There are those who want everyone to be at the same level. That does not work either. It kills all incentive and puts all the power in the hands of a few government storyteller leaders.

Some people have investigated the earnings of our government leaders over their careers. They tend to report exponential earnings over their tenures, far above what an above average person achieves. Those earnings do not appear to coincide with the salaries paid to them. Wikipedia reported the average salary for Senators and Congressmen at $174,000 per year in 2022[18]. Even if they invested the entire amount and got an average rate of return of 8% per year the total would be just under 9 million in 20 years. Many have started out like most people with mortgages and hoping they earn enough to meet the bills. Now they may be mega millionaires or even billionaires. I know it can happen if someone comes up with a good idea and then creates a company to market it, but the government is not anyone's company. They are all employees. I am not pointing fingers at anyone. It just seems odd that the company (the government) is going deeper and deeper in debt while the employees are reaping incredible wealth.

The Bible is clear that all men are sinners and government leaders cannot be trusted any more than ordinary citizens. We have already seen what happens. That is exactly what happened in Nazi Germany. Rights were trampled on, people persecuted, and power was all in the hands of a few led by a fanatical leader.

The President, Vice President, and members of Congress are all elected officials. They are chosen by the people and in theory, are responsible to the citizens of this nation. If God exists, then they are also responsible to God. Those positions carry a certain amount of authority. Everyone in authority must remember that they are also under authority. Elected officials are accountable to those who put them in the office. It is an honor to be elected. Should taking responsibility, humility, and civility be the hallmark of all who seek those positions? Should elections be focused on issues and solutions and not on personal attacks? Perhaps we might consider term limits

---

[18] Wikipedia, Salaries of Members of the United States Congress, April 9, 2022.

for Congress like we have for the President. It might check the egos and keep those in office reminded that the citizens of the United States put them there.

Consequences

The choices we make all have consequences. Good ones produce good results, bad ones bad results. Some of the choices often have unexpected consequences for us and others.

Free

Free, we hear that word a lot. Actually, though, nothing is ever free; someone always has to pay. If someone steals from someone else, the injured party suffers a loss. If the loss is covered by insurance, the insurance company takes the hit. If not covered and others try to help, then those others absorb the loss. Someone always pays.

There are consequences to the thief also. If he justifies stealing, he is setting the rules for how people can act toward him. He cannot steal and then say it is unfair to steal from him. Now he will have to resort to some form of power to maintain control over what he has stolen. That only works until someone more powerful than him comes along. It is an endless cycle. If God is there, He is watching.

There is also the normal business interaction, where people buy and sell. Companies are in the business to make money, which means they have to sell their products at a price higher than their costs. Those costs include labor, costs related to the product, facilities costs, shipping, advertising, etc. If any of these costs go up, the company either has to improve efficiency or raise the prices. That is why we pay over 10 times as much for gas or a car today than when I first bought one in the early 1970's.

There are ads on TV all the time telling those who have been exposed to such and such a chemical to call a number because they may be entitled to some compensation. That isn't free either. The chemical companies facing such lawsuits have to pass on those costs as price increases for the products still on the market. Lawsuits against drug companies produce the same results. Malpractice suits increase the costs of medical services. It is frightening what a stay in the hospital costs these days. It will eventually get to a point where no one will be able to go to a doctor or a hospital. Insurance will cost too much. The government isn't going to be able help; they are already broke. It just seems that the lawyers are all vying for who can get the client the most money, whether it is justified or not does not seem to be relevant.

Insurance

Insurance is also a product and when costs go up so do the rates. Car insurance goes up because cars cost more and cost more to repair. It also goes up because of accidents. It goes up when drivers do not obey the laws and think they have the right do anything they want any time they want. It isn't rocket science. Some areas of the country where accident rates are high will generate higher costs.

Medical insurance rates are climbing for the same reason; it costs more for hospitalization, drugs, and doctors. Lifestyles also contribute to the increase in costs. It is known, for example, that smoking is linked to cancer, heart disease, and a host of other medical problems. Those with alcohol or drug problems also contribute to the increase in costs. Obesity is linked to heart disease, diabetes, and other problems. Almost anyone can reduce the number of medications they take simply by losing excess weight and eating better. Even my grandmother in her eighties got herself off insulin for diabetes by losing weight and changing her diet. I am no different. As I write this, I am about 20 pounds overweight; Ok, 30 pounds. A typical bowling ball weighs about 15 pounds. That means that everything thing I do, every place I go I am carrying around two bowling balls around my belly. If I picked up 2 bowling balls and carried them around everywhere it would be obvious the effect on my body. Because we are not physically carrying excess weight in our arms, however, we tend to ignore the physical strain on us. There are stories and ads all the time about people losing incredible amounts of weight, 50 pounds (over 3 bowling balls), 100 pounds (almost 7 bowling balls), etc. I saw an ad where one person lost 235 pounds! That is almost 16 bowling balls! I cannot fathom how that person was even able to function with that much excess weight.

There is another consequence as well; when I shower and look in the mirror, I do not like the way I look. I want to cover up that bulge around my stomach, so I wear "tent" clothing, oversized shirts over my pants to cover up my belly. When I wear such clothing, I have the illusion that people do not notice the excess weight. I suspect others feel the same way and spend a lot of money on clothes, cosmetics, and perhaps other things in a vain attempt to make themselves look good. My time and energy may be better spent just eating better and losing weight.

Please do not misunderstand me. This is not a condemnation of bigness. I saw a man on TV that was absolutely ripped. His arms were bigger than my thighs. He was huge but I think you would have trouble finding an ounce of fat on him. He looked like he could bench press 600 pounds or more. He looked good! He admitted he liked to eat and cook. He worked out, though, and ate healthily. It showed. That is the difference. He exercised regularly, converting fat into muscle. He now could handle a higher calorie intake. He balanced his love of eating with a lot of exercise. I suspect he did not need a lot of medications.

No one really has the right to dictate our lifestyles but at the same time, is it really fair to expect others to pay the price for those choices? Should those who work hard eating heathy food and keeping their weight down be forced to pay increased premium insurance costs due to a large segment of the population that is overweight for example?

There is another lifestyle choice that also affects medical costs, sex. The Biblical position is that a man should leave his father and mother and cleave to his wife in a monogamous relationship for a lifetime (Genesis 2:24, Exodus 20:14). If this pattern is followed, it is almost impossible to acquire a sexually transmitted disease. The chances drastically increase with multiple partners. Many years ago, AIDS became a big concern. That one disease spawned a host of medical tests and devices to detect and monitor that disease. Once the AIDS virus was detected in an individual, their immune system would have to be continually monitored, possibly for the rest of their lives. All of those tests cost money. In addition, the pharmaceutical companies have spent huge amounts in attempts to cure or curb the disease. How much money would have been saved in medical expenses if we all had just followed the Biblical plan?

Finding solutions for the rising costs of health insurance is not a single party issue; it is a national issue. Simple solutions may not be possible. There are too many variables contributing to the costs. The government is already too heavily in debt to just pick up the tab for those costs and doing so does not solve the root problems. Would it be better to determine the reasons for those rising costs and then seek solutions to reduce them? Reducing the costs, for example, to develop new drugs and bring them to market should lower the cost of those drugs to the patient. Like all businesses, management people make the most money and the skilled workers make the least. It is the skilled workers such as nurses that are the most critically needed people in hospitals. What if the salary schedule favored the critical workers the most and management was secondary, would that help to reduce costs with better patient care? In any case, our leaders should seek real solutions and not political gains. In the end though, all of us may have to accept that it is going to cost more. Discounts for insurance might be granted to those whose individual choices and lifestyles make them less prone to health problems. Why should those who do not smoke, keep their weight down, exercise regularly, do not engage in promiscuous lifestyles, etc. have to pay for those with increased risks? Should the government find ways to reward good practices instead of protecting bad behavior and habits?

The point of all of this is that choices have consequences. If we do not prepare for life's changes, we may find ourselves destitute and a burden on families and our nation. If we refuse to work, why should anyone feed us? Shouldn't everyone pay their fair share?

Our Founding Fathers set God and the Bible as the standard. When the nation of Israel followed God's standard, it went well with them. When they sought other standards (other gods), God became angry and withdrew from them. Then they were conquered, captured, or killed (examples: *Judges, Isaiah, Jeremiah*). Haven't we done the same thing? We only seek and worship God when we are in deep trouble. Then we have the audacity to say "where was God" when tribulation comes. God is not obligated to bless us when we rebel or come running to our aid when fall into deep trouble. Choices have consequences. God may choose to allow those consequences to play out rather than rescue a person, group or even this nation. He allowed the nation of Israel to be taken into captivity for seventy years by Assyria under Nebuchadnezzar. These were God's chosen people!

We have made our government like a god, replacing the God of the Bible. We rally around one person or another. They tell us stories or make promises. They are not God, though. They are often not experts. Are those promises real or are they just blowing in the wind? Can the government fix bad choices or solve problems by spending more money they do not have? Can we defend liberty throughout the rest of the world when we are slaves financially to the very nations that are the bullies of the world?

Only God has the power to change things, but He will not act unless we repent.

Repentance

Individually: Each person needs to recognize that they are sinners before a Holy God.

For all have sinned and fall short of the glory of God. (Romans 3:23)

What do we get for that sin?

For the wages of sin is death,.. (Romans 6:23a)

Recognize that Jesus died to pay the penalty for our sin.

But God demonstrates His own love toward us, in that while we were yet sinners, Christ died for us. (Romans 5:8)

We need to repent, and individually believe in the gospel.

..Jesus came to Galilee, preaching the gospel of the kingdom of God, and saying "The time is fulfilled, and the kingdom of God is at hand, Repent, and believe in the gospel."(Mark 1:14b-15)

What is the gospel?

For God so loved the world that He gave His only begotten Son, that whoever believes in Him should not perish but have everlasting life. (John 3:16)

Chapter 8
Conclusion

The Founding Fathers of our country faced an enormously daunting task to birth a new nation. They chose to, even had to reach for wisdom far beyond their human experience. They witnessed the depravity of man in history through self-aggrandizing despots. They saw the cruelty that men inflicted on others. They realized that they could not even rely on religious institutions to be free from it. Witch hunts occurred not that long before in history. Kings often ruled through the church by telling people what to believe. They even saw the sin in each other as tempers flared in debating the issues. They rejected the wisdom of story tellers and chose to reach instead for God and His Bible.

The fear of the Lord is the beginning of knowledge, but fools despise wisdom and instruction. (Prov 1:7)

They knew that they could not trust future generations to always do right. They had seen the rise of benevolent kings that brought peace for a while only to have that peace shattered by foolish inheritors of that power. Even the Bible was full of such examples. Moses was a strong God-fearing leader. The minute he was absent for a while the people followed storytellers and built a golden calf and made it a god. David and Solomon built up the nation of Israel to its greatest glory under God. Israel was later broken and eventually brought into captivity under a ruthless pagan nation.

They knew the lure of sin. They knew the seduction of pride and power on the good intentions of men. They had to build a system of shared power so that no one person or group could seize total control. They also knew that people out of fear, anger, or some other strong emotions were prone to follow whatever charismatic storyteller that happened along to fuel that emotion. They needed to protect dissenters that stood against the flow of the masses following the pied piper storytellers. They tried to balance power with individual rights. It would all be for naught though if there was no greater power than themselves to preserve the fragile nation. They felt that only God could preserve the young nation. It would be in God they would trust.

While ancient Israel was to be hospitable to aliens in their midst and treat them well, they were not to incorporate those pagan rituals and beliefs into their nation. They knew it would anger God and remove His blessings from them. The aliens must accept and assimilate into the Jewish nation, not the other way around. God and His Law was to guide them. When Jesus was asked what the greatest commandment was, He responded:

> *"...You shall love the LORD your God with all your heart, with all your soul, and with all your mind. This is the first and great commandment. And the second is like it: You shall love your neighbor as yourself, on these two commandments hang all the law and the Prophets. (Matt 22:37-40)*

Today, we see evidence that our nation is running away from God. People are being led away by a new generation of storytellers that are revered as experts. God is being replaced with mere men. It's easy to see the fear of our Founding Fathers. Can this nation survive if the protecting Hand of God is removed? Perhaps not!

Good is now being called evil and evil good. Families are being torn apart. Violence is rampant. Mass murders seem to be occurring all the time. Children are not safe in their own schools. In some cities, there are armed guards outside the stores. Riots are becoming all too common. Those that simply disagree with those in power are ostracized and labeled as hate mongers. Politicians no longer seem to civilly debate issues. The goal seems to be which party can find the most dirt on their opponents and disgrace them. Would the Founding Fathers be in tears if they could see what has happened to their precious United States of America? Would it drive them to their knees in prayer for God to heal this land? God has promised:

> *If My people who are called by My name will humble themselves, and pray and seek my face, and turn from their wicked ways, then I will hear from heaven, and will forgive their sin and heal their land. (2 Chronicles 7:14)*

At the end of Jesus' most famous sermon, The Sermon on the Mount (Matt 5-7), He cautioned his listeners:

> *Therefore, whoever hears these sayings of Mine, and does them, I will liken him to a wise man who built his house on the rock: and the rain descended, the floods came, and the winds blew and beat on that house; and it did not fall, for it was founded on the rock. But everyone who hears these sayings of Mine, and does not do them, will be like a foolish man who built*

his house on the sand: and the rain descended, the floods came, and the winds blew and beat on that house; and it fell. And great was its fall. (Matt 7:24-27)

Was the Founding Fathers' efforts to seek the guidance of God and the Bible true **Wisdom**?

The fear of the Lord is the beginning of knowledge, but fools despise wisdom and instruction. (Prov 1:7)

There is a way that seems right to a man, but its end is the way of death. (Prov 14:12)

www.ingramcontent.com/pod-product-compliance
Lightning Source LLC
Chambersburg PA
CBHW022102020426
42335CB00012B/801